UTOPIA AND REFORM IN THE ENLIGHTENMENT

UTOPIA AND REFORM IN THE ENLIGHTENMENT

FRANCO VENTURI

Professor of Modern History
University of Turin

CAMBRIDGE
AT THE UNIVERSITY PRESS
1971

Published by the Syndics of the Cambridge University Press
Bentley House, 200 Euston Road, London N.W.1
American Branch: 32 East 57th Street, New York, N.Y.10022

Library of Congress Catalogue Card Number: 71–123676

ISBN: 0 521 07845 8

Printed in Great Britain
at the University Printing House, Cambridge
(Brooke Crutchley, University Printer)

CONTENTS

INTRODUCTION

It is certainly a great responsibility to be invited to give the George Macaulay Trevelyan Lectures, but it is an equally great pleasure to spend three weeks in Cambridge, with so many friends and colleagues and amid its libraries. The result of the invitation is contained in this book. Although the problem I have chosen is evidently wide-ranging, I hope the points of view from which to observe its aspects will prevent too much dispersiveness, and permit me to touch on at least some of the central questions of the great age of the Enlightenment, in its difficult yet fruitful equilibrium between utopia and reform.

I was tempted to entitle these George Macaulay Trevelyan Lectures: 'Was ist Aufklärung?' However, I resisted this temptation, not through fear that I might be accused of wishing to be considered on the same level as Immanuel Kant, Moses Mendelssohn, and other scholars who, in 1784, replied to this question posed by the 'Berliner Monatsschrift'. I hope that no one has misgivings about my own capacity for self-criticism, at least in this field. If I have not gone back to the initial data of the debate on the Enlightenment, it is because I am convinced that that debate, however interesting, has always risked leading research away from its proper path.

From Kant to Cassirer and beyond, our understanding of the European Enlightenment has been dominated by the philosophical interpretation of the German *Aufklärung*. At least Cassirer was sincere and entitled his book *Die Philosophie der Aufklärung*. Let us have a look at it.

Limiting ourselves to Germany, we see that Baumgarten and Bodmer, Jerusalem and Lessing, Wolff and Kant dominate. Schlötzer and Büsching, for example, are not found here. Yet the former was the most important 'publicist' of the second half of the eighteenth century. He revealed to German eyes an entire historical world, that of Russia, and, better than anyone else, showed the difficulties and obstacles confronting liberal thought in the Germany of that age. The latter gave a new dimension to geography. His books dominated their field in Europe. There is not one economist to be found in the whole of Cassirer. An *Aufklärung* which does not mention the state, the land, or commerce, is clipped in at least one of its wings. As Diderot said: 'Imposez-moi silence sur la religion et le gouvernement, et je n'aurai plus rien à dire.'[1]

It is true that Cassirer talks a lot about eighteenth-century religion. But about government, not as juridical theories but as politics, he says little or nothing. And this tendency shows no sign of changing among historians of the Enlightenment. In 1968 an important book was published in Italy, *L'illuminismo tedesco. Età di Lessing*, by Nicolao Merker.[2] The author is a Marxist. He continually discusses the social value of philosophical ideas. But Schlötzer and Büsching are hardly mentioned, while the German physiocrats appear never to have existed. Everything is there, from religion to society. What is lacking is 'le gouvernement', as Diderot said—concrete political action.

A careful examination shows that the philosophical interpretation of the *Aufklärung*, from Kant to Cassirer and on to present-day scholars, may well be a misleading factor in various ways. This happens because it involves a kind of history which always tends essentially to trace things back to their origins, to the first beginnings of the ideas which it sees at work in the reality of the eighteenth century. It looks back to Descartes, to Leibniz, to Locke, to Malebranche, to Vico; it sees in them the sources of those thoughts which were later used and blended by popular philosophy, which were taken up in the course of the ideological struggle during the century of the Enlightenment. How are we to put our house in order after this battle? The only thing to do is to see how the concepts which lie before us, broken and twisted, were born; how those arms which we must now refurbish on the whetstone of a great philosophical system were made, on one of the great concepts of the world—rationalism, naturalism, sensism, etc. What a pity it is that this method runs counter to what was the fundamental character of Enlightenment thought, that is the firm determination not to build philosophic systems, the complete distrust of their validity. Half way through the century Condillac, Voltaire, Diderot and d'Alembert stated this with the utmost clarity. Evidently we must not follow the ideas back to their origins, but examine their

[1] *La promenade du sceptique* in *Œuvres complètes*, Paris, 1875, vol. I, p. 184.
[2] Bari.

function in the history of the eighteenth century. Philosophers are tempted to push upstream until they arrive at the source. Historians must tell us how the river made its way, among what obstacles and difficulties. From the end of the eighteenth century onwards, many Germans were tempted to give a mythical value to the source, and to seek there every good and all light. Whenever I, too, am tempted to trace history backwards in order to explain an idea or an event, I turn again to that passage by Herder, which seems to me to be valid for all time as a caricature of Germanic nostalgia for the *Ur*, the origins, the sources. 'How delightful it is when we read a poetic account of the origin of each single thing; the first sailor, the first kiss, the first garden, the first death, the first camel.'[1]

Historians of the Enlightenment should never lose sight of this caricature. Herder was merely naive when he wrote these lines in his fragment on the *History of the lyric*, shortly before re-examining and deepening this vision in his pamphlet of 1774, *Auch eine Philosophie der Geschichte*. But subsequently, the flight to the past to explain the present has become more and more refined and complicated. It is not so easy to recognize this nostalgia for the *Ur* when it is decked out in the most alluring arguments, but it remains just as dangerous. We are no longer faced with such simple things as the first garden of humanity, the earthly paradise and its patriarchal inhabitants, but, let us say, the Augustinian and theological *civitas dei*. As we know, *The heavenly city of the eighteenth-century philosophers* is the title of a famous book by Carl Becker.[2] Enigmatically, the author presents his book to the reader thus: 'This certainly isn't history. I hope it is philosophy, because if it is not it is probably moonshine: or would you say the distinction is over-subtle?'

One is not surprised to learn that the Italian followers of Croce liked this book, with its attempt to fuse history and philosophy in the Enlightenment.[3] But the result is misleading. It derives from an effort to find in the thought of Diderot, or d'Holbach, Voltaire and Hume, *not* what was new, historically important and fruitful, but

[1] *Versuch einer Geschichte der lyrischen Dichtkunst* in Herder, *Sämtliche Werke*, edited by Bernard Suphan, Berlin, 1891, vol. 32, p. 89.

[2] New Haven, 1932.

[3] On Becker and Croce, see Burleigh Taylor Wilkins, *Carl Becker. A biographical study in American intellectual history*, Cambridge, Mass., 1961, pp. 193 ff.

what substantially coincided with the fundamental ideas of the past, natural law, moral philosophy, immortality. This is retrospective history, told with great charm and scholarship, as always happens with intelligent conservatives. They are sceptical about everything, except their own determination not to yield to the new, the unexpected, to anything outside their heavenly city. Carl Becker's book was published in 1932. Since then, it seems to me, every study of eighteenth-century Europe has borne witness to how much of the eighteenth century really remains outside the walls of the *civitas dei*. One might even say the Enlightenment itself. Carl Becker remains an important episode in the history of American conservatism and culture. But, every year, his *heavenly city* has receded more and more into an isolated concept, far from the work of those who have tried to trace the course of eighteenth-century history.

Yet the temptation to look back is evidently strong, and not easy to resist. One of the most open critics of Carl Becker is Peter Gay. It is he, more than anyone else, who has given us a critical and realistic vision of Voltaire's political thought, a vision not blurred by philosophical and ideological schemes. Yet when he wanted to give a subtitle to his work *The Enlightenment: An interpretation*, he could find nothing better than, *The rise of modern paganism.*[1] It is hardly necessary to say how important this work is. It is the greatest attempt so far to synthesize all that has been said and thought on the eighteenth century in these last decades. Yet the first volume, in its very construction, reveals this insistent search for origins, for the recovery of the past. There is an *ouverture* to *The Enlightenment in its world* in the *Troupeau des philosophes*, that is, on the problems of the diffusion of the new thought in Europe, and of the relationship between the small group and the social structures and forces of the age. At this point, one might expect an account of the formation of the *troupeau*, and of what it really did in its context. But, instead, we find *The appeal of antiquity*, *the useful and beloved past.* We find Hebrews and Greeks, Pagans and Christians. And then, at last, we think we have got to the end. The last part of the book is called *Beyond the holy circle.* Here we meet d'Holbach and Diderot; but behind them, there still looms the great shadow of Lucretius. *The mission of Lucretius* ends the first

[1] New York, 1967.

volume of this work, so full of interesting and important things, yet such a clear proof of how difficult it is to break the magic circle of the tradition of the German *Aufklärung*, the vision of the Germanic *Humanität* at the turn of the eighteenth century and the beginning of the nineteenth, the passion for Greece and Rome which grew in the universities of Germany. As I closed this book, I thought of Delio Cantimori, my friend who recently tragically passed away, one of the men for whom the age of humanism ended with the French revolution. He too enclosed in an ideal world scholasticism and the humanists (up to the dawn of the Enlightenment, from Petrarch to Rousseau, as he once wrote).[1] In the valuable *Bibliographical essay*, at the end of the first volume, Peter Gay himself gives a clear statement of his points of departure and reference: Cassirer first of all, the Warburg Institute, Fritz Saxl, Auerbach. Peter Gay brings a modern philosophical sensibility to this tradition. For example, he is much more aware than Cassirer ever was of the value of eighteenth-century materialism. He has a political sensibility which the German humanists traditionally lacked. But these are new branches grafted on to an old and glorious trunk. Peter Gay's book could really be called *Was ist Aufklärung?*, not such a small compliment.

I myself have tried to make a limited, but I think useful, test of the humanist point of view in the interpretation of the eighteenth century. I have tried, that is, to understand the exact meaning of the answer Kant himself gave to that question. His answer, as everyone knows, is the motto of the Enlightenment: *sapere aude*. They are Horace's words. What better proof could there be of the presence of the ancient world, or even, as Peter Gay asserts, of the identification of the men of the Enlightenment with pagan antiquity? One remembers again the lines of Voltaire, the words of Diderot, the essays of Galiani on Horace. We could go on through all 'enlightened' Europe, finding the Latin poet everywhere.

But what does this presence mean? This doubt was borne in on me a long time ago. When I was a youth, Gaetano Salvemini used to speak to me about Horace with great admiration, almost with veneration. It was my good fortune to know personally this man of the

[1] *Valore dell'umanesimo* in *Studi di storia*, Turin, 1959, p. 383. Cf. also *idem*, *Il problema rinascimentale a proposito di Armando Sapori*, Turin, 1959, pp. 366 ff.

Enlightenment, living in the twentieth century. I remember how astonished and puzzled I felt, though, of course I did not dare say so, that he, Salvemini, could love the poet of the age of Augustus. How could a man of such independent and frank character, whose political ideas were so emancipated, whose social conscience so acute and modern, how could a scholar of his stamp venerate Horace, politically and socially so different, even his opposite? Was it the magic of poetry? This answer didn't satisfy me then, and it doesn't now; not for Salvemini, not for Diderot, or Voltaire. My doubt grew still more the day I heard Francesco Saverio Nitti declare that if I wanted to be an historian I should always bear in mind the profound maxim of Cicero, that history was eloquence and oratory. Nitti was not a student of the Enlightenment, but he was certainly an enlightened economist. I now live in Italy, a country where, if a young man wishes to enter university to study, let's say, the history of the Russian intelligentsia, or of the European working-class movement, he must attend a high school where he will be obliged to read, not only the poems of Horace in Latin, but also those of Anacreon in Greek. Yet it was in Italy that the eighteenth-century advocates of the Enlightenment, great and small, were beginning to criticize the compulsory teaching of Latin in addition to their criticism of the law and of the Roman tradition.[1] Evidently classicism has won, for reasons which need not be examined here. In fact, it is certain that the relationship between the humanist tradition and social and political realities of the modern world is much more complex than it might at first seem. But the survival of the ancient world may *not* be a presence, an identification, as Peter Gay maintains. It is often an ornament, not a reality, a superstition, not a religion.

The little test of *sapere aude* seems to me fully to confirm this.[2] The motto is certainly Horatian, taken from Epistle II, book I, *Ad Lollium*, line 40:

[1] The most vigorous pages are those of Luca Magnanima, *Lettere italiane sopra la Corsica*, Lausanna (actually Leghorn), 1770, letter XVII, reproduced in *Illuministi italiani*, tome VII, *Riformatori delle antiche repubbliche, dei ducati, dello Stato pontificio e delle isole*, edited by G. Giarrizzo, G. Torcellan and F. Venturi, Milan–Naples, 1965, pp. 828 ff.

[2] F. Venturi, 'Contributi ad un dizionario storico. "Was ist Aufklärung? *Sapere aude*"' in *Rivista storica italiana*, 1959, I, pp. 119 ff.

> Dimidium facti, qui coepit, habet: sapere aude,
> incipe...

Dacier's translation renders the sense well: 'Ayez le courage d'être vertueux.'[1] He adds in a note: 'Pour aspirer à la sagesse il faut du courage et ne pas se rebuter par les difficultés. C'est pourquoi Horace dit *aude*, ose...' The motto begins to acquire a different sense when it is considered in the light of the Christian and theological conception, and tends to suggest a contrast with the words of St Paul: 'Noli altum sapere, sed time.' Grotius used it in a purely humanistic sense, as an exhortation to study seriously. But when Pierre Gassendi used it, he transformed, as Luigi Firpo observed, 'the Horatian saying into a conscious appeal for freedom of enquiry, infusing the ancient words with all that lucid tension of a seeker after essential truths which was naturally his'.[2] But we are still in the phase of *libertinisme érudit*, of a libertinism wrapped in a Christian mantle. Before entering the world of the Enlightenment *sapere aude* has to pass along very different roads.

We are no longer in the world of scholars, but in the smoke-filled rooms of the Society of Alethophiles, where the thought of Wolff begins to ferment in this typical confraternity of churchmen, officials and lawyers of the Prussia of Friedrich Wilhelm I. Johann David Kohler tells us how Ernst Christoph von Manteuffel in 1736 caused a medal to be struck in Berlin. It showed an armed Minerva. Amid the plumes on her helmet are the heads of two philosophers, Leibniz and Wolff, and written around it are the words: 'Sapere aude', 'Erküne dich vernünfftig zu seyn' in a contemporary translation.[3] That year, Kohler tells us, Berlin became the capital of the philosophers. Von Manteuffel was the inspirer of the Alethophiles, a politician and adventurer whose friends called him, more simply, 'le diable'. The statute of the Alethophiles, the *Hexalogus alethophilorum*, tells us the society was based on an explicit determination to spread the truth, to organize its supporters, to constitute, by means of solidarity and mutual help, a pressure group. The political ferment is evident, and already appears in an embryonic way to secure the triumph of truth.

[1] André Dacier, *Œuvres d'Horace*, Paris, 1727.

[2] L. Firpo. 'Contributi ad un dizionario storico. Ancora a proposito di *sapere aude*' in *Rivista storica italiana*, 1960, I, p. 117.

[3] Johann David Kohler, *Historische Münz-Belustigung*, Nürnberg, XII, no. 47, 23 November 1740, pp. 369 ff.

Before reaching Kant, the *sapere aude* of the Alethophiles still had a long way to go, and I cannot claim to have rediscovered all its steps. Another medal was struck in 1765 at the request of Stanislaus Augustus Poniatowski. It clearly shows how widespread this motto was, even though it takes us back to a more traditional and humanistic world. In fact, it was struck to honour Stanislaus Konarski, the famous Piarist who did so much to create a new culture and a new education in Poland. For him, the Horatian motto was paraphrased and adapted: *sapere auso*—thus dedicated to a man who had been able to adopt and observe the motto *sapere aude*.[1]

The original motto can be found, a few years later, in *De cultibus magicis* by Konstantin Franz de Cauz, published in 1767, a book in which the author resumed and codified the struggle of Tartarotti and Maffei against witches and magicians and of Van Swieten against vampires. The decrees of Maria Theresa against both these sinister phenomena had marked a turning-point of fundamental importance in the relations between the eighteenth-century states and popular superstition. In this work *sapere aude* became the true motto of enlightened despotism.[2]

A year later, in 1768, it reappears on the frontispiece of the German translation, by Christian August Wichman, of Shaftesbury's *Characteristicks*; almost a link between the *Aufklärung* and English deism.[3] When Kant published his article, in 1784, the motto had become common usage. In 1788, four years after this article, we find it once more on the frontispiece of a book, published at Frankfurt and Leipzig *Geschichte der päbstlichen Nunzien in Deutschland*, one of the many works by Friederich Karl von Moser. The book is an ample and confused attack on Catholicism. It interprets the Protestant reformation as a struggle against obscurantism; there is also clearly present an element of German patriotism. In a sense, with all its polemics against everything which happened in Italy, it was a veritable overthrowing of any humanistic mentality, in the name of the Enlightenment and incipient national pride.

[1] Władysław Konopczyński, *Stanisław Konarski*, Warsaw, 1926, p. 63, and Jean Fabre, *Stanislas-Auguste Poniatowski et l'Europe des lumières*, Paris, 1952, p. 67.

[2] F. Venturi, *Settecento riformatore. Da Muratori a Beccaria*, Turin, 1969, pp. 385 ff.

[3] *Charakteristicks, oder Schilderungen von Menschen, Sitten und Zeiten, aus dem Englischen übersetzt*, Leipzig, 1768.

Over almost two centuries, from Gassendi to Kant and beyond, the Horatian words had been applied to the most diverse, even opposite things. But this motto's journey through time was certainly not governed by chance. There was an historical link between Grotius and Gassendi, Manteuffel and Konarski, Shaftesbury and Kant and Von Moser. Here we see the logic which led from the rationalism and free-thinking of the seventeenth century, from the original spreading of masonry in Europe in the 1720s and 1730s, to the work of the enlightened monarchs in Poland and Austria in the second half of the eighteenth century, from the reflections of philosophers such as Kant to the outburst of political passions at the end of the century. *Sapere aude* had accompanied this historical logic, but it certainly did not create it, neither did it profoundly modify it. As Kant rightly said, this was the motto of the Enlightenment. Our little test, I hope, has not been useless. Following these vicissitudes, we have pin-pointed some of the essential stages in the movement of the Enlightenment. I believe we have also measured the distance from the classical world, from ancient Epicureanism, and the poetry of Horace to the reality of the eighteenth century. Horace and his motto *sapere aude* have been a dream of philosophers, a consolation for those who felt themselves increasingly involved in the battle of the Enlightenment, a lament for a lost world and a mask to conceal ideas which were too bold and dangerous. In reality, it has not helped us to understand the deeper logic of the Enlightenment, even though it has revealed, here and there, the emergence and the changes in its ideas and moods.

When one considers the uncertainties and difficulties which face the historian of ideas, it is hardly surprising that a different and to some extent an opposite approach has been sought. This approach starts from society and not from ideas, from groups and not from individuals, from climates of opinion not from elements in the thought. It uses the techniques of sociology and economic history. In this way, it tries to understand the Enlightenment by constructing schemes, tables and diagrams, searching for its real and hidden meaning in the general development of the eighteenth century.

Like all historiographic attempts, this has had and still has its paradoxical and absurd aspects. If one takes a modest and peaceful French provincial academy of the eighteenth century, and draws a multitude of arrows shooting off in all directions into Europe just because one of its members happened to live in Florence or elsewhere; if one produces a diagram more closely resembling the battle of the Marne than an academic structure, one is obviously using a cyclotron to crack a nut. To be more specific, I am alluding to the article by Daniel Roche, entitled 'L'Académie de Châlons-sur-Marne', published in *Annales* in 1964.[1] But let us ignore these curiosities and consider studies in which there is a greater harmony between means and ends.

Naturally, this social history of the Enlightenment has a Marxist character. But it doesn't try to understand the content, origins and development of the Enlightenment which might help to explain Marxism itself, or, more generally, the rise of the economic, political and social ideas of the last two centuries of our modern age. On the contrary, it attempts a reverse operation, that is, it tries to explain the Enlightenment in the light of the writings and opinions of Marx, Engels and their school. The pity is that the history of German or Russian thought between the years 1830 and 1870, or the more recent ideological currents of the last thirty years of this century, would gain by a new and good interpretation of the internal rhythm and development of the European Enlightenment in the eighteenth century, comparing the elements of revolt and faith, of hope and disappointment. The Marxist view, however, does not generally lead to this comparison. It tends to see the Enlightenment as part of the Marxist vision and to apply its own schemes to its interpretation.

Karl Marx, Engels and their followers have certainly written interesting and acute things on Diderot and the French revolution, Lessing and Gianmaria Ortes. Thus we can always learn from their approach, but, of course, we must not consider it the only one; nor should we forget to compare their findings with what we can learn from Herzen, Cattaneo, from Michelet, Jaurès, Salvemini or from Keynes. But Marxists generally do not see things this way. They claim to give an overall interpretation of the Enlightenment. Their claim is founded on the belief that the thinkers of the Enlightenment represent a stage in the development of bourgeois ideology. I am convinced that this definition is one of the obstacles in the way of a deeper under-

[1] 'La diffusion des lumières. Un exemple: l'Académie de Châlons-sur-Marne' in *Annales*, 1964, v, pp. 887 ff.

standing of the eighteenth century, and that this hypothesis must be abandoned if we wish to make progress more easily and rapidly. It is true that the Enlightenment or certain aspects of it became at one time instruments of defence and attack in the struggle against the survival of the feudal, aristocratic, medieval world in France, Spain, Italy and elsewhere. It is equally true that this function was not always and everywhere the task of the Enlightenment. The historian must discover how and when and to what extent this did happen. He must never accept a pre-established identification. If he does, he runs great risks. In France, for example, he may fail to comprehend the opposition to Louis XIV, the controversy of Dubos and Boulainvilliers, the rise and significance of Montesquieu, the importance, which was also ideological, of the struggle of the parliaments, of the so-called rebellion of the nobility, etc. In Italy, he would risk failing to understand the character of the Enlightenment of groups such as those of Count Verri, of the Marquis Beccaria, of the Marquis Longo, etc. So he would probably not understand the Enlightenment of the *Accademia dei Pugni* in Milan. This latter group was composed entirely of aristocrats with one exception, and he was an ecclesiastic, Father Frisi. As a social group it would have fitted perfectly into the society of the old regime. In southern Italy, the example of Filangieri may be sufficiently significant. I believe that, wherever one looks, the relations between the bourgeois forces, however active or static, and the movement of the Enlightenment, must remain a problem; they cannot be taken for granted or used as an historical presupposition.

The *enfant terrible* of contemporary French Marxism, Lucien Goldman, seems to know this very well. He has attempted to give an even more absolute and general value to the connection between the Enlightenment and the bourgeois, at the risk of ending up in absurdity. 'It seems to us, that the link between the Enlightenment and the bourgeois has a *fundamental* character, even though it may seem to have disappeared in the periods of crisis in bourgeois rationalism, such as the advent of German idealism and in the years between 1914 and 1945. We must add that even in these periods of crisis, rationalistic conceptions do not completely disappear, as may be seen, for example, in the work of Valéry, where the subservience to rationalism is accompanied by an awareness of its crisis.'[1] Clearly we are faced with an historical phenomenon which is subject to eclipses. We could hardly have a better caricature of this way of reasoning than this: the idea of Valéry as the guiding light of the rationalist bourgeoisie in the thirty years between the two wars, in the age of Marc Bloch, of Einstein, Freud and Croce.

It is these ideological statements, lacking any historical content, which help us to understand why there has been a reaction in France and elsewhere. This reaction has led scholars to seek a social interpretation of the Enlightenment which is still more or less tacitly inspired by Marxism, but resolutely decided not to carry whatever intuitions it provides to absurd lengths. They base their enquiries on effective social reality and precise historical research.[2] A very good example of this approach is provided by Jacques Proust's book, *Diderot et l'Encyclopédie.*[3] The French middle classes of the middle of the eighteenth century are divided into a series of groups and forces which are anything but homogenous. The *Encyclopédie* is not in the least studied as a sort of overall uniform expression of the various positions it contains. There is no comparison between a hypothetical encyclopaedical spirit and the reality in which it operates: on the contrary, the real position held by each of the encyclopaedists in the society of his time is studied in detail and with critical rigour. The men of the church, and of the parliament, the noblemen and writers, and the artisans who contributed to the great dictionary are closely examined. Jacques Proust tries, for example, to investigate concretely the nature of the effective relations between Diderot and the *ateliers*, between Diderot and the technology of his time, between Diderot and contemporary artisans and workers. His conclusions are patiently constructed on a statistical foundation, and they are clear: the encyclopaedists constituted a small *élite* of learned men and experts. They are associated with economic life as leading factors in economic progress, and are also closely connected with the administrative and governmental apparatus which they tried to improve and make more

[1] *L'Illuminismo e la società moderna. Storia e funzione attuale dei valori di libertà, eguaglianza, tolleranza*, Turin, 1967, pp. 98–9.

[2] Aldo Garosci, *Sul concetto di 'borghesia'. Verifica storica di un saggio crociano* in *Miscellanea Walter Maturi*, Turin, 1966, pp. 437 ff.

[3] Paris, 1967.

rational. In short, Diderot is a reformer. His collaborators in France correspond to those *élites* which were one of the two indispensable elements in every enlightened despotism, and which provided the new mentality in the courts of Maria Theresa, Peter Leopold, Friedrich II and Catherine II. 'Bourgeois, certes, les encyclopédistes le sont tous ... Mais non de grands bourgeois... Ils n'appartiennent pas non plus à cette petite et moyenne bourgeoisie qui représentera si bien la sans-culotterie et d'où sortiront les pionniers de la révolution industrielle. Juristes, médecins, professeurs, ingénieurs, hauts fonctionnaires civils et militaires, savants, techniciens spécialisés, ils se situent exactement à mi-chemin de la grande et de la moyenne bourgeoisie, assez proches des couches sociales les plus élevées—et assez bons juges de leur incapacité—pour aspirer à les suppléer dans leur rôle dirigeant traditionnel, mais non pas si loin du peuple travailleur qu'ils ne pussent avoir une vue précise des problèmes réels qui se posaient à la nation. Ils étaient enfin bien placés pour concevoir la solution technique de ces problèmes et pour la mettre quelquefois en œuvre sans attendre une révolution générale.'[1] There is a definition which sums up this painstaking description: 'Les technocrates en tout genre qui étaient les encyclopédistes.'[2] Here we clearly see the limits to which Jacques Proust's analysis can be carried. He has succeeded in defining the encyclopaedists not in terms of their class, but of their function, not in terms of social history, but in terms of political history. The encyclopaedists are not such because they are situated between the high and the petty bourgeoisie, but because they created certain technical instruments of action in the French society of the middle of the eighteenth century. We are back with 'le gouvernement' of Diderot, with concrete political action. In this case, let us consider the definitions of their contemporaries. They called them the party of philosophers, or, sometimes, a sect or a movement. These definitions are still more true and precise than the modern schemes. What can be added by a subtle, learned, social analysis? Jacques Proust certainly dedicates a large part of his book to the study of Diderot's political ideas and to the internal struggles and the contrasts within the group of the encyclopaedists. But both these aspects are less alive, less historically meaningful because they are considered as

[1] Proust, *Diderot et l'Encyclopédie*, p. 505. [2] *Ibid.* p. 509.

expressions of a mentality, as reflections of a social situation. They are not considered directly as revealing the difficult and even dramatic choices these men had to make. They are not considered as leading to action, as elements in an historical narration, but as the figures and schemes of a social diagram. The use of the term 'technocrat' serves wonderfully well to reveal what is uncertain and equivocal in such a position, half-way between history and sociology. Are the technocrats really a party masquerading behind their technique, or are they experts obliged by force of circumstance to assume a political role? Wouldn't it be better to return to the interpretation of the encyclopaedists as *philosophers* and reformers, as people who lived for their ideas, and who found a way of changing the reality which surrounded them? The book by Furio Diaz, *Politica e filosofia nel Settecento francese* seems to me to be on the right track.[1]

So it is not enough to refine and soften the Marxist inspiration. How can one avoid considering, for example, the problem of the success of reform in some countries in eighteenth-century Europe and the repeated failure of enlightened despotism in France? This is a political and historical problem which no sociological method will ever solve.

The risk of a social history of the Enlightenment, especially evident in France today, is that ideas may be studied when they have already been worked out and accepted and established and so become 'structures mentales'. The moment of active creation slips by unobserved. The whole 'geological' structure of the past is examined, but not the soil in which the ideas themselves germinate and grow. Historiographically the result is often to confirm, with a prolific display of new methods, what we already knew, what had already come to light through the struggles of the times and the reflections of historians. For example, it is my sad belief that at least a part of the research carried out on eighteenth-century books and magazines by the *Sixième section de l'École des Hautes Études*, under the direction of Alphonse Dupron, risks falling into this category. *Livre et société dans la France du XVIIIe siècle*[2]—it would be hard to imagine a more attractive title for an historian of the Enlightenment. He will willingly forgive that touch of Pythagorean mysticism to be found in these pages. The

[1] Turin, 1962.

[2] G. Bollème, J. Ehrard, F. Furet, D. Roche, J. Roger, *Livre et société dans la France du XVIIIe siècle*, Post-face d'A. Dupront, Paris–La Haye, 1965.

reader is constantly distracted from his consideration of concrete results and invited to bow down before the religion of the contemplation of numbers. However well-disposed he may be, doubt begins to creep back when he sees François Furet, after an enquiry into book production in France, carried out with surveys and a wealth of research, conclude as follows: 'importance des belles lettres et mantien des grands genres', 'permanence des livres de droit', as well as 'grand mouvement séculaire inverse des ouvrages de religion et de "Sciences et Arts"'. His conclusion is: 'Il s'agit aussi bien de l'observation technique, de la réforme d'un abus, que de la reconstruction de la cité; toute une montée sociale s'exprime à travers le double langage de l'expérience et du rêve.' We can see that numbers are set aside in the conclusions, in order to bring to the fore those truths which all the history of the ideas of eighteenth-century France had already taught us. A similar thing happens when Jean Ehrard and Jacques Roger count the foreign books reviewed in the *Journal des savants* in 1715–19 and then in 1750–4. They reach the surprising conclusion that, while in the first period the number of Italian works is almost negligible, in the second, they are more numerous than those arriving from the German speaking countries, from Switzerland, and even from England. They are second only to books published in Holland.[1] Really this mystery is not so difficult to solve. From 1750 to 1754 the *Journal des savants* reviewed the eight volumes of the *Annali d'Italia* by Ludovico Antonio Muratori. Such figures do not make reality any clearer, but must, in their turn, be explained by facts which are more easily observable. But I shouldn't like to carry these criticisms too far. Sometimes numbers really do seem able to reveal long-standing faults. In Italy students are crammed with the history of historiography. To us it seems curious that, for example, Alphonse Dupront is so struck by the fact that the number of history books remains substantially the same throughout the eighteenth century. He would have expected to see it increase after Voltaire's *Essai sur les mœurs*. 'Littéraires à merci, nous pensions volontiers que la poussée de l'histoire était fin de siècle, après Voltaire et plus proche des plongées préromantiques aux abîmes du temps passé.'[2] But Muratori, Maffei and Vico belong to the first part of the century. And Augustin Thierry has taught us that

[1] G. Bollème *et al.*, *Livre et société*, pp. 37 ff. [2] *Ibid.* p. 195.

modern historiography of the third estate and of the nobility begins with Dubos and Boulainvilliers in France as well.

Almost nothing remains of the Marxist inspiration. What does remain, however, is both the most important and the most dangerous element. It is the pretension of creating a total history, a vision of society as a global structure able to reveal its inner logic, the laws governing its own existence if it is submitted to a suitable interpretative instrument, whether it be the class struggle, quantification or structuralism. This claim to discover *le mot de l'énigme* of a civilisation may be more or less evident and explicit. It always carries with it the risk of distorting historical judgments by transforming them into a philosophy of history, if not, as Carl Becker observed, into 'moonshine'.

Thus, the more useful studies in the social history of the Enlightenment are still those which bring ideas and facts into close contact within precise and clearly defined sectors, which study the diffusion of certain discoveries of science and technology, and see how they act in country and in town, between the nobles and the artisans of this or that country. The last ten years have seen the publication of several outstanding models of such research. One need only recall Michael Confino's *Domaines et seigneurs en Russie vers la fin du XVIIIème siècle. Étude de structures agraires et de mentalités économiques*,[1] Marc Raeff's *Origins of the Russian intelligentsia. The eighteenth-century nobility*.[2] (I have mentioned these two authors, because their opinions differ. Their argument in the pages of *Annales* is of great interest for all students of the history of eighteenth-century Russia.)[3] Also important are the three large volumes by André Bourde, *Agronomie et agronomes en France au XVIIIe siècle*.[4] The concreteness and wealth of detail in this work make the reader wonder how important the new agricultural techniques really were in the effective transformation of French agriculture. Last but not least, one should mention the contributions to the great debate now being conducted in England on the impact of ideas, plans and ideologies on the eve of the industrial revolution.[5]

[1] Paris, 1963. [2] New York, 1966.

[3] Michael Confino, 'Histoire et psychologie: à propos de la noblesse russe au XVIIIème siècle' in *Annales*, 1967, pp. 1163 ff. [4] Paris, 1967.

[5] Peter Mathias, *The first industrial nation. An economic history of Britain, 1700–1914*, London, 1969.

Books like the one by Charles Wilson on the seventeenth and eighteenth centuries make one hope that other scholars will follow this track in other European countries.[1] These are well-known examples and they suffice to show how the social and intellectual history of the eighteenth century is being renewed and reinvigorated.

I greatly admire these and similar historians. I may even feel a certain envy of them and certainly feel a constant desire to learn from their books. Yet, in these G. M. Trevelyan Lectures, I should like to remain faithful to my youthful aspiration, when I planned to write a political history of the *Encyclopédie*. I shall not dare to follow the steps of Alfred Cobban, nor shall I accept his invitation to discuss *The role of the Enlightenment in modern history* itself, the subtitle of his book *In search of humanity*.[2] (How moving it is to turn to his pages again after his recent death.) I certainly don't claim to offer a *Geschichte der abendländischen Aufklärung*, as Fritz Valjavec has done.[3] Regarding the history of ideas in the eighteenth century I should like to throw a little light here and there. My central concern will be to try to put the problem of the impact of the republican tradition on the development of the Enlightenment. This will lead to the very heart of the question of utopia and reform, which I shall study from a single and significant point of view: the right to punish. The conclusion will be an attempt to see the geographic distribution and the rhythm of development of the Enlightenment in eighteenth-century Europe. I hope to be able to show that these problems, however different they may seem, really do converge in a political history of the Enlightenment.

[1] *England's apprenticeship 1603–1763*, London, 1965.

[2] London, 1960.

[3] Vienna–Munich, 1961.

I

KINGS AND REPUBLICS IN THE SEVENTEENTH AND EIGHTEENTH CENTURIES

WHEN WE SPEAK of the republican tradition and of the importance of its role in forming the political ideas of the eighteenth century our mind at once turns to the ancient world, and to the great examples of Athens and Rome. Of course, the importance of the classical tradition is beyond any doubt. What I should like to do now is not so much to measure its intensity and importance in the eighteenth century or to see how it was used in the age of the Enlightenment. I shall not enquire into how much republican thought derives from Pericles or Titus Livius, but rather how much derives from the experience undergone by the Italian, Flemish and German cities, by Holland, Switzerland, England and Poland. The republican tradition which the eighteenth century inherited and made fruitful sometimes had a classical colouring. More often it was born from a direct experience, and one not so distant in time. It was a root which came to life again after the age of absolutism and the restorations of the sixteenth and seventeenth centuries.

It is by no means accidental that the ancient and classical form of republican thought was particularly evident in France in the last decades of the century, until the time when it began simmering dangerously during the revolution. The *philosophes*, the Girondins and the Jacobins, looked to Camillus and Brutus for the very reason that the French had no experience which could serve as a model of republican inspiration. They attempted a rethinking of the past, of the medieval cities, of Étienne Marcel and of the freedom of their Frankish forefathers. But if they wished to seek not simply examples of virtue but also free forms of organization and constitution, they had inevitably to turn to Athens and Rome. But for the whole of the eighteenth century they, too, derived strength from the English, Polish, Italian and Dutch examples. As we shall see, for them also the roots of republican thought, from Montesquieu to Rousseau, were deep in a European experience which was recent and not at all mythical. But these examples did not belong to them directly; they were less local, less 'personal'. For them only the neo-classical model could assume the grandeur and vigour of a myth. Thus it was France which restored an ancient form to the European republican tradition.[1]

This is very evident in Italy at the end of the eighteenth century. One has only to compare the political thought of the age of the enlightened reformers, let's say between 1734 and 1789, with that of the revolutionary age in the last decade of the century. One immediately notes a rift, a notable difference in vocabulary, in the modes of feeling and expression. Eighteenth-century Italy had been profoundly anti-Roman. It had supported the provinces against the capital. It had rediscovered and exalted the Italic peoples who had existed before the conquest, the Etruscans, the Insubrians and the Samnites. It had fought the idolatry of Roman law. It had deeply criticized an economic system founded on conquest and not on trade. It had been able to appreciate the distance which separated the liberty of the ancients from that of their contemporaries. The French revolution and the subsequent invasion of Italy overlaid this critical ferment with a very different stratum. Brutus, Camillus and the others were to come alive again on Italian soil, where, in fact, they were well and truly dead and buried. Jacobin propaganda, monotonous and exalting at the same time, brought into Italy a republican ideal which was ill-suited to a country in which the republican experience was firmly rooted. The classical forms became a weapon with which to destroy a tradition. Ancient Rome was not conjured once more into existence by this return to the ancient world. However, the republics of Genoa, Venice and Lucca were either profoundly transformed or swept away. The age of the single and indivisible republic arrived in a country where

[1] On the historical vision of antiquity, in the eighteenth century as well, in all Europe, cf. Arnaldo Momigliano, *Contributo alla storia degli studi classici*, vol. I, Rome 1955, vol. II, Rome, 1960, vol. III (with the title *Contributo alla storia degli studi classici e del mondo antico*), Rome, 1966, vol. IV, Rome, 1969. On the religious vision, Frank E. Manuel, *The eighteenth century confronts the gods*, Cambridge, Mass., 1959. On the psychological and artistic aspect, Jean Seznec, *Essai sur Diderot et l'antiquité*, Paris, 1957. For further bibliographical information, Peter Gay, *The Enlightenment: An interpretation*, pp. 455 ff. On the political aspect, the least studied, cf. H. T. Parker, *The cult of antiquity and the French revolutionaries*, Chicago, 1937.

republics had been many and in constant movement, both internally and externally. If we wish to retrace the republican tradition which has its roots in the Middle Ages and in the Renaissance, both in Italy and Europe, we must, therefore, explore the past beyond the Jacobin and neo-classical stratification.[1]

The example of Italy itself may be particularly instructive. At the beginning of the eighteenth century the peninsula is a sort of microcosm of all Europe. Not even Germany offered such a great variety of political forms and varying constitutions, if only because the papal theocracy was exclusive to Italy. The country was a real political museum with monarchies, dukedoms and republics, from Venice to the little community of San Marino.

The value of the Italian republics as an example has been vigorously affirmed by the historiography of the Enlightenment and of the romantic period; one need only recall Sismondi. Subsequently the study of their social and economic aspects seems to have ousted the study of their political and constitutional experiences. However the interest of these latter has been pointed out recently by a man who is an acknowledged master in economic and social history, Frederick C. Lane, in an article confirming a whole new line of study in the Italian Republics.[2] The discussion of Venice in Italy has been ample and fruitful in recent years (one has only to remember the name of Gaetano Cozzi). It has been widely taken up abroad and has now been critically re-examined with great clearness and ability by William J. Bouwsma,[3] while the relationship between politics and society is described very well by Marino Berengo in his *Nobili e mercanti nella Lucca del Cinquecento*.[4] On the contrary, the history of Genoa still has to be considered from a point of view which goes beyond local tradition.[5] Naturally Florence and Tuscany remain exemplary for whoever wishes to understand the

[1] Compare, for example, the texts published in the collection of the *Illuministi italiani*, vols. III, V, VIII, Milan–Naples, 1958, 1962, 1965, with those collected by Renzo de Felice in *I giornali giacobini italiani*, Milan, 1962.

[2] Frederick C. Lane, 'At the roots of republicanism', *American History Review*, 1966, n. 2, pp. 403 ff.

[3] W. J. Bouwsma, *Venice and the defence of republican liberty. Renaissance values in the age of the Counter-Reformation*, Berkeley, 1968. We recommend this also for its very complete bibliography.

[4] Turin, 1965.

[5] For a study of this, see Vito Vitale, *Breviario della storia di Genova*, Genoa, 1955.

relationship between the Italian communes and the formation of the modern state. It is enough to remember the works of Frederico Chabod, Hans Baron, Giorgio Spini and Nicolai Rubinstein and to recommend the recent discussion and bibliography contained in Marvin B. Becker's *Florence in transition.*[1] In contrast with Sismondi many of these writers on the Italian republics end with the close of the Renaissance, which is prolonged to a greater or lesser degree into the first decades of the seventeenth century. One often notices a tendency to regard the survival of the republics into the age of absolutism in the seventeenth and eighteenth centuries as a 'myth'. However, their continued existence has an importance greater than that of a memory or a myth. The formation and the increasing of the modern state may well be illuminated if we look at it not from the point of view of the victorious monarchies, but from that of the republics surviving with such tenacity.

On the whole the relationship between absolutist states and republics was the same as the relationship prevailing in the rest of Europe. Genoa, Venice, Lucca and San Marino had survived on the borders of modern states. They had a strange relationship with these states, which might have seemed almost parasitic, but which had become solid and irremovable. It is true, of course, that Spain had done its best to overthrow Venice, as it had done when trying to conquer the United Provinces. It is true that the dukes of Savoy had made a great effort to conquer Genoa. The Tuscan Grand Duchy had often been tempted by Lucca. As late as 1739, the Papal State had made a last attempt to put an end to San Marino.[2] Yet, in spite of the variety of circumstances, the great disparity of political situations, in spite of the wide range of religious affiliations, which included Dutch Protestantism, Venetian jurisdictionalism veined with sympathy for reform, and the baroque and bigoted Genoa, the absolutist states were never able to eliminate their opponents and enemies. The ancient republics survived.

During the sixteenth and seventeenth centuries the republican states had conducted themselves as separate and external structures.

[1] Baltimore, 1967 and 1968.

[2] On the paradoxically significant case of San Marino, see the most interesting book by Aldo Garosci, *San Marino, mito e storiografia tra i libertini e il Carducci*, Milan, 1967. This work is at the origins of many of the considerations made here on the republican tradition in the modern age.

Their social nature was aristocratic and patrician, bourgeois and municipal. They resembled those other structures which the monarchies were then trying to dominate and to incorporate inside the absolutist state, not through destruction but through submission, of the parliaments, the state assemblies, the rule of the urban nobility, military and political organizations of Huguenots in France, numerous local and city autonomies and privileges of old cities. The whole process of the formation of the modern state comes to mind as we contemplate these long-standing contrasts and compromises. The republics are the same structurally, but external and separate. Their existence may sometimes appear as dubious and formalistic as that of the political forms within the absolute state. In reality, Genoa is included in the Spanish world. The patrician cities of Switzerland occasionally seem to have no more independence than *Franche-Comté* or the Alsatian cities, absorbed by the French advance. Yet the external structures survived, and, in continental Europe, kept the republican tradition alive. It was they who preserved an alternative model to monarchy, and denied the latter its final triumph, not only on the political and military level, but also on the ideological.

One of the most important historiographical discussions of the last twenty years, a truly international debate, has concerned the re-examination of the relationship between the forming of the modern state and the social structures which were being subdued and absorbed. One need only read the papers of Fritz Hartung and Roland Mousnier,[1] of J. Vicens Vives[2] and of Erik Molnar,[3] as well as the collection of articles in honour of B. B. Kafengauz, edited by N. M. Družinin.[4] Particularly stimulating is a book by Ernst Heinrich Kossman, who sees the absolutist state, halfway through the seventeenth century, as the 'résultat d'une neutralisation, non pas d'une unité'.[5] 'Il est une somme

[1] *Quelques problèmes concernant la monarchie absolue* in *X Congresso Internazionale di scienze storiche. Relazioni* vol. IV, *Storia moderna*, Florence, 1955, pp. 3 ff. This is recommended also for its bibliography.

[2] *Estructura administrativa estatal en los siglos XVI y XVII*, in *XIe Congrès International des sciences historiques. Rapports*, vol. IV, *Histoire Moderne*, Stockholm, 1960, pp. 1 ff.

[3] *Les fondements économiques et sociaux de l'absolutisme*, in *XIIe Congrès International des sciences historiques. Rapports*, vol. IV, *Méthodologie et histoire contemporaine*, Vienna, 1965, pp. 155 ff.

[4] *Absoljutizm v Rossii (XVII–XVIII vv.)*, Moscow, 1964.

[5] *La Fronde*, Leiden, 1954.

de mécontentements et de forces contradictoires qui se contrebalancent.'[1] He notes, quoting Dubosc Montandré, how at that time in France the danger of an 'esprit républicain et contagieux'[2] was not absent, but how, in fact, the faint republican flame which had been lit at Bordeaux with the movement of the Ormée was soon extinguished amid the political contradictions which appeared among the ruling classes, between the bourgeoisie and the people and between the various social forces and the foreign allies. Kossman has the advantage of being able to consider such events bearing in mind the existence of a republican alternative, that of Holland.[3]

How the ancient republics kept the republican tradition alive in continental Europe was very evident when France under Louis XIV took up with renewed energy the struggle which Spain was no longer able to conduct. The Dutch war of 1672 and the bombardment of Genoa in 1684 open a new chapter in the conflict between the absolutist states and the ancient republics. This chapter was concluded in 1748 with the peace of Aix-la-Chapelle. After those eventful years the survival of the United Provinces, once again invaded by France, was assured. So was that of Genoa which only a revolt and a hard war had been able to save from the hands of the kingdom of Sardinia and of the Empire.

In this long and decisive phase from the seventeenth to the eighteenth century (1672 to 1748) the republics had again seemed specially vulnerable. Their neutralism, their conservatism, their attempt to flee from political conflict to the world of commerce and banking, their rejection of militarism in favour of finance, their determination to keep constitutions which appeared ill-suited to withstand the onset of the monarchies, all seemed certain to bring about their downfall. Yet this did not happen. The onset itself caused internal upheavals again. In Holland, it re-awoke the conflict between the regents and the house of Orange and between one province and another. Holland reached the brink of disaster and ruin. Then, not only were the United Provinces saved, but also the essential parts of their constitution. William III and William IV came very close to being kings, but, in fact, remained stadtholders. The danger, ever present from 1672 to 1747, brought

[1] *Ibid.* p. 260. [2] *Ibid.* p. 108.

[3] For the second part of the seventeenth century cf. Lionel Rothkrug, *Opposition to Louis XIV. The political and social origins of the French Enlightenment*, Princeton, 1965.

them to power. They were supported by the nobility, the army and the unruly people. But the constitutional framework inherited from the past did not collapse. The patriciate of the regents continued to hold the key positions in the society of the Low Countries.[1] Religious toleration was never questioned. On the contrary, its continued existence enabled Pierre Bayle and the other French emigrants to make Holland the emporium of political, philosophical and scientific ideas for the whole world. Fifty years later Marc-Michel Rey in Holland became the publisher of the *philosophes*.

The United Provinces had remained a republic. They had retained, politically, a form of government which was considered abnormal, strange and increasingly incomprehensible by those whom the absolutist state was amalgamating and enclosing. The consciousness of this diversity became more and more firmly rooted in Holland. Peter Cornelis de La Court's book is its most typical expression. It was published under the title of *Mémoires de Jean de Witt*, and was read everywhere in Europe. The German edition of 1671 opened with the motto: 'Pax optima rerum. Solae respublicae veram pacem et felicitatem experiuntur...' It then alludes to the resolute application to economic affairs of the government of the United Provinces: 'Ita industria et labore Batavorum respublica locupletatur.'[2] The argument against monarchies was explicit and vigorous. The English edition is a good example. It was published in 1702, a year in which, as we shall see, the republican form of government was once more advocated. The desire of the republics for the welfare of their citizens was contrasted with the desire for power and expansion of the monarchies. It was asserted that 'the inhabitants of a republick are infinitely more happy than the subjects of a land governed by one supreme head'. It was not a case of an 'angelical or philosophical republick' similar to the model of Plato, Aristotle or to the 'Eutopia Mori', but an example of a

[1] D. J. Roorda, *The ruling classes in Holland in the seventeenth century* in *Britain and the Netherlands*, edited by J. S. Bromley and E. H. Kossman, Groningen, 1964, pp. 109 ff. 'Even after 1672 the monarchical and aristocratic tendencies did not fuse. In many respects William III, however great the power, remained the prisoner of the oligarchy' (p. 132).

[2] *Anweisungen der heilsamen politischen Gründe und Maximen der Republicen Holland und West-Friesland*, Rotterdam, 1671. For the relations between de La Court and Spinoza, cf. the preface and the comment by Antonio Droetto to the *Trattato politico*, Turin, 1958.

prosperous state, based on a 'common interest wonderfully linked together', on tolerance, freedom of immigration and trade, on the absence of monopolies, on the moderation of the taxes and on the will to remain at peace, even at the cost of considerable sacrifice.[1] The very mentality of *raison d'état*, which the Italians practised, was repudiated. They could theorize about policies in which the lion and the fox had equal parts; they, too, could constantly repeat: 'Con arte e con inganno / si vive mezzo l'anno / Con inganno e con arte / si vive l'altra parte.' These were not maxims for richer and more populous countries such as the republics, which were more similar to agile and prudent cats, rather than big and violent lions. They were ready to defend themselves tooth and claw, but only if their existence was threatened. 'A cat indeed is outwardly a lion, yet she is, and will remain but a cat still, and so we who are naturally merchants, cannot be turned into soldiers.'[2] War could not and should not change the nature of the republic. The stadtholder would remain an arm of defence under the control of the merchants, not a prince or a king. Amid the lions and the tigers which dominated the world, the foreign policy of this exceptional animal which was Holland was bound to reveal a natural sympathy for its fellows, who also existed for peace and commerce. The other republics would be its natural allies. De La Court speaks of Venice with esteem and admiration. He looks with interest at the other Italian republics and at those in Germany. Yet he is obliged to conclude that, from a military point of view, they are too weak, while economically they are more rivals than allies. They are of little or no use in the struggle for survival, against the 'innate hatred which all monarchs bear to republicks'.[3] However, they are good examples of the constitutional errors which must be avoided at all costs. The magistrates of the republic must not be paid. Their income must come from commerce, from manufacturers, but not from the state. No law or privilege, such as majorat, should defend them: 'Thus it is still, or was lately in the republicks of Venice, Genoa, Ragousa, Lucca, Milan, Florence...'[4] There must not be a permanent head either at the centre, or in the city and local administrations. The determination

[1] La Court, *The true interest and political maxims of the republick of Holland*, pp. 15, 37 ff.
[2] *Ibid.* pp. 244–5.
[3] *Ibid.* p. 287.
[4] *Ibid.* p. 375.

not to change the system of government must prevail over every other exigency, otherwise economic and political ruin will ensue. Commerce, navigation and manufactures settled and continued in Italian republics so long as they enjoyed their liberty. 'But we may easily perceive that Florence and Milan, tho they became the courts of monarchs or stadtholders did much decrease in their commerce during the monarchical government. Pisa..., all the old great Italian cities since the loss of their free government...are fallen almost to nothing...Whereas those two ill-situated towns, Venice and Genoa, by their free government, notwithstanding the loss and removal of Indian trade, have preserved their greatness and traffick as much as possible, and little Lucca keeps her trade still.'[1] The destiny of the Hanseatic cities which had remained free and independent was similar. The whole of Dutch political thought during the seventeenth century tends to formulate the religious, psychological, and juridical conditions of such a survival, and follows the parallel destiny of the other, smaller European republics with constant attention.[2]

Modern research into the commercial, manufacturing and financial vicissitudes of Holland in the seventeenth and early eighteenth centuries, the impassioned discussion of these recent years on the character and significance of the decay of the United Provinces in the eighteenth century have increasingly revealed, from the point of view of economics too, the particular character of the republic of the United Provinces. Just as in politics it refuses to accept the *raison d'état*, so, in economic matters, it rejects mercantilism. Its function as merchant and banker to the great modern states, in the very age of their consolidation, renders it both vulnerable and indispensable, parasitical and indestructible. What might seem to be a decline is really a tendency towards stasis in a world in which England and the

[1] La Court, *The true interest and political maxims*, p. 432.

[2] E. H. Kossman, *Politieke theorie in het zeventiende-eeuwse Nederland*, Amsterdam, 1960. The most thoroughly worked out juridical theory of the aristocratic republics in the seventeenth century is that by Ulrich Huber, *De iure popularis, optimatium et regalis imperii sine vi et a sui iuris populo constituti*, 1689. It contains frequent parallels between Venice, Florence and the 'Batavorum respublica', 'ubi summa potestas est penes *ordines*, hoc est equites et civitatum rectores, verissima aristocratia' (p. 50). Interesting thoughts are to be found in Charles-Irénée Castel de Saint-Pierre, *Projet de traité pour rendre la paix perpétuelle entre les souverains chrétiens*, Utrecht, 1716 and also *Annales politiques*, London (Paris), 1756.

continental states are growing and developing. With the second half of the eighteenth century Holland's difficulty in adapting itself to a changing world becomes more and more evident. Its economy is as unreformable as its political structure. In 1751, the proposals of the stadtholder were not taken up. However acute the crises of 1763 and 1773, they are still not decisive. Holland fell only when it too was overwhelmed in the upheavals of the modern revolutions from the 1780s onwards. As long as the old regime endured, the republic of the United Provinces survived.[1]

Genoa and Venice in the years of transition from the seventeenth to the eighteenth century still await an historian who will do for them what English and Dutch scholars from Pieter Geyl to Charles Wilson and Kossman have done for Holland. Of course the Italian patrician republics in their decline are not nearly so important politically, intellectually and economically as the United Provinces. One need only recall William III, de Witt, Rembrandt, and Spinoza. But their instincts of self-preservation, their continued existence on the borders of absolutist states deserve a closer look. To some degree they too helped to form the idea of the republic which the men of the Enlightenment had.

Genoa was bombarded by the French in 1684, and occupied by the Austrians in 1746. Both these events stimulated social movements again in a society which had become more and more stratified since the sixteenth century. The dukes of Savoy had already tried to exploit the poverty of the people to conquer Genoa. They had even been so openly demagogic as to call for a revolt against the poor and scarce black bread which the people were obliged to eat, and against the economic and fiscal monopolies possessed by the ruling nobility.

Giovanni Ansaldi, the agent of Carlo Emanuele I, published two pamphlets at the time of the Vachero plot: *Verità esaminata a favor del*

[1] Charles Wilson, *Anglo-Dutch commerce and finance in the eighteenth century*, Cambridge, 1951 (reprinted 1966); *idem*, *Profit and power. A study of England and the Dutch wars*, London, 1957; *idem*, 'The decline of the Netherlands' in *Economic History and the Historian, Collected essays*, Cambridge, 1969, pp. 22 ff.; I. Schoffer 'Did Holland's golden age coincide with a period of crisis?' in *Acta historiae nederlandica* I, Leiden, 1966, pp. 82 ff.; J. De Vries, *De economische achteruitgang der Republiek in de achttiende eeuw*, Amsterdam, 1959; Johannes Hovy, *Het voorstel van 1751 tot instelling van een beperkt vrijhavenstelsel in de Republiek*, Groningen, 1966 (where one also finds interesting parallels with the contemporary free port policy at Hamburg and Genoa).

popolo, il quale con ingiustitia è tenuto fuori del governo di Genova contro alcuni tiranni dell'istesso popolo che già se ne credono impossessati con fraude,[1] and especially, *A tutto l'ordine fortissimo, fedelissimo, generosissimo che intende reprimer le insolenze e ripararsi dalle ingiustitie di quelli che male operano e male governano in Genova, salute e aviso,*[2] 'The truth examined on behalf of the people who are unjustly kept out of the government of Genoa, against certain tyrants of this same people who already believe they have taken possession of it by fraud.' 'To all the strong, faithful and generous order of men who intend to put an end to the insolences and avenge the injustices of those who badly conduct themselves in Genoa, greetings and a warning.' In this latter, the author addresses himself to those who govern the public and wonders: 'did they found Genoa without our forefathers?' 'The government of our city has always been in the hands of those who were most powerful, although it really should have belonged to all.'[3] With the help of the duke of Savoy, who would not be the lord of Genoa, but its 'protector', all those who did not belong to the aristocracy could and should rebel. 'I may well affirm that the hundred and fifty thousand in the cities and all the people along the coast...should be able at least to defend themselves against those few who until now have oppressed us.'[4] The mercenary troops, Germans and Corsicans, would not suffice against this insurrection; 'we do not need many factions to tackle our problem, let's all agree for one whole day not to go to the Banchi (the commercial centre of the city), let the artisan class be content to take a holiday on the same day. Let the common people throw their putrid and stinking bread at the heads of those who give it them to eat, and on that same day perhaps we shall begin to turn over a new leaf without taking up any weapons. Let's begin by saying that we do not wish to be so ignorant in all our classes and groups as to be willing to pay taxes, duties, excise, or other vexations, to support unjust wars, and to keep guards who treat us badly, to fill the city with gendarmerie who torment us and protect them and that finally we do not intend to give salaries to those who govern us so badly.'[5] The *Second Aviso* is also interesting. It was published after the execution of Vachero and his accomplices. We find curious information

[1] N.p., 1628. [2] N.p., 1628. [3] *Ibid.* p. 9. [4] *Ibid.* p. 9.
[5] G. Ansaldi, *A tutto l'ordine fortissimo*, p. 13.

in it about the religious and political life of Genoa. It concludes: 'How could the people be subjugated more, even if we lived under the dominion of the Turks? How can the people become any poorer than these tyrants have made them?...the poor man must eat rubbish, the artisan is considered to be a slave.'[1]

In the 1680s, France, under Louis XIV, had made a much more concerted and enterprising attempt to dismember the old republic. The French acted from the top downwards. They tried to use the more ancient feudal families, the Fieschi, for example. At the same time, they tried to win over the more recent nobility, together with the bourgeois, the merchants who were not noble (i.e. the social class which had continued to exist and develop in the shadow of the privileges of the aristocracy after the crystallization caused by the constitution of Genoa in 1576). In other words, they tried to make use of the same forces which were the basis of the power of the crown in France, from the nobility drawn to the court, to all those who had succeeded best in maintaining their position in the absolutist state by means of the acquisition of offices and the mercantilist policy pursued by Colbert. The report of Pidou de Saint-Olon, the French emissary to Genoa in those years, which was rightly admired at the time, is enough to show us how skilfully the absolutist state of Louis XIV tried to exploit the internal contrasts of the ancient republic, and how it tried to carry out the same policy of penetration which had so often succeeded in France, and with social forces which were similar in many ways.[2]

The discussion on how to conquer Genoa by taking advantage of the internal conflicts of that republic became intense in France from the beginning of the eighties of the seventeenth century. This can be traced in the despatches and records of the time. Thus: 'quand on coupe la tête à une république le reste du corps est perdu, ce qui n'est pas dans un état monarchique'.[3] It was therefore first thought necessary to strike at the ruling aristocracy. Saint-Olon, in 1683 and 1684, urged the government of Louis XIV not to rely too much on the struggles within the aristocracy between 'ancient' and 'new' nobility, but to

[1] *Ibid.* pp. 13–14.
[2] Vito Vitale, *Breviario della storia di Genova*, vol. I, pp. 308 ff.
[3] Paris, Archives des Affaires Étrangères, Gênes, 16 (1681), pp. 401–13.

direct their efforts above all towards the bourgeois, the wealthier merchants, who saw they were excluded from government even though they were no less rich and powerful than a part, at least, of the aristocracy. The common people, the workers, should not be taken into account. They were tied to the Spanish policy, and to the trade with the Iberian peninsula and Sicily. They fully participated in the traditional Genoese freedom, however poor and turbulent they might be.[1] Colbert's fierce hatred for 'that rabble of Genoa', and his determination 'to ruin the nation's commerce and prejudice its public dignity, and finally to oppress its liberty' is noted in the despatches of De Marini, the Genoese representative in Paris.[2] The latter also told of the growing animosity in Paris against the Genoese nobility,[3] and a year later, from the prison of the Bastille, warned his government of the extent to which France was trying to bring about 'a great alienation of the people from the nobility and from the government'.[4]

The violence and the bombardment of the city in 1684 brought results which were just as negative as those of the war against Holland. Genoa remained in the Spanish sphere of influence. The act of homage and contrition which Gianfrancesco Imperiale Lercari was obliged to make at Versailles was certainly a grave humiliation. But it did not put an end to the existence of the republic.[5] This was exactly what the Genoese aristocracy wanted, whatever damage had been done to their city by the cannons of Admiral Duquesne in the name of Louis XIV. Duquesne was a Huguenot, and the bombardment took place on the very eve of the revocation of the Edict of Nantes. To endure, to survive—this was the profound determination of Genoa. It was the republican form of government which made such a policy possible. The governing classes knew it. Like the Dutch, they were sure they could survive wars and destructions as long as the essential character of their patrician and urban constitution was not changed. 'Let the republic be eternal, and princes mortal', as Giovanni Paolo Marana

[1] *Ibid.* Gênes 19. The Papers of Pidou de Saint Olon at the Bibliothèque de l'Arsenal nos. 4760, 6546 and 6613 should also be seen.

[2] State Archives of Genoa, Lettere Ministri Francia, no. 2202, January 1683.

[3] *Ibid.* 2 July 1683.

[4] *Ibid.* no. 2203, of 20 September 1684.

[5] Filippo Casoni, *Storia del bombardamento di Genova nell'anno 1684*, edited by Achille Neri, Genoa, 1877.

had written.[1] The important thing was not to yield. 'Je l'avoue — je l'avoue, je découvre tous les jours que mon mal est plus grand que je ne pensois et que mon peuple est épuisé. Les charges sont excessives, le commerce est ruiné, les artisans ne font rien et toute la ville est ensevelie dans une profonde douleur. Il faut pourtant avoir bon courage, et ne faire aucune lâcheté. Je suis résolue de m'ensevelir sous mes ruines, comme Numance', as Marana made Genoa say in his *Dialogue de Gênes et d'Algers*.[2] Marana affirms that at Genoa, too, the danger had induced some people to think it was necessary for all powers to be concentrated in the hands of a few, that it was vital to put an end to the long-standing balance and allow one of the magistracies to gain the upper hand over the others. Genoa continues: 'J'ai pensé plusieurs fois, dans mes conseils, de donner une autorité absolue à la redoutable magistrature de mes Inquisiteurs d'état, de faire assassiner et empoisonner qui qu'il leur plairoit, sans aucune forme de procès, pour faire périr tout ceux que par leurs actions ou leurs discours font paroître quelque inclination pour la France.'[3] These Machiavellian plans, the sinister dreams of a threatened aristocracy, were attributed by Marana to Lercari, the doge, the man who had to make the formal act of homage to Louis XIV. But they were never put into practice, and, in any case, the emergency policies still remained in the context of the existing magistracies. But the shadows of a dictatorship which would transform itself into a monarchy were not far away. 'Car enfin quel malheur plus grand peut arriver à un état que d'estre gouverné par un homme qui s'imagine d'estre plus sage que tous les autres?... Pour ce qui est du peuple il feroit bien des choses s'il avoit un chef,

[1] *La congiura di Raffaello della Torre, con le mosse della Savoia contro la Repubblica di Genova, libri due. Descritta da Giovanni Paolo Marana*, Lyons, 1682, p. 71.

[2] *Dialogue de Gênes et d'Algers, villes foudroyées par les armes invincibles de Louis le Grand l'année 1684, avec plusieurs particularitez historiques touchant le juste ressentiment de ce monarque et ses prêtensions sur la ville de Gênes, avec les responses des Génois. Traduit de l'Italien*, Amsterdam, 1685, p. 93. See also the Italian text: *Dialogo fra Genova et Algieri città fulminate dal Giove gallico*, Amsterdam, 1685.

[3] Marana, *Dialogue*, p. 112. There is no lack of evidence that for some time at Genoa the necessity of concentrating the power in the hands of a few had been contemplated. 'The architecture of the government of the republic is not suitable for dealing with the state negotiations, and if juntas with few members able to deal easily with politics are not instituted, everything will go to rack and ruin.' One may read this in a *biglietto di calice* of 14 July 1673, Genoa, State Archives, Politicorum, bundle 14, no. 1660, f. 14. On the extension of the powers of the state inquisitors in the years of the bombardment, see *ibid.* bundle 16, no. 1662, ff. 45 ff.

mais il n'ose rien entreprendre parce que je veilles dedans et dehors...' The risk that a stadtholder might become a prince is present in Genoa as in Holland, but Genoa knows it too, and can and will resist. In fact Marana sees only one way out of the crisis, in spite of so much republican pride. Genoa would never live in peace beside its powerful neighbour, France, until: 'les nobles, qui l'ont gouvernée avec tant d'insolence, d'ignorance et d'injustice soyent bannys à perpétuité ...reléguez dans l'isle de Corsique qu'ils ont rendue déserte, et condamnez à la cultiver et à estre les sujets du peuple, comme perturbateurs du repos public, ennemis des bons citoyens, infracteurs des loix divines et humaines et scandaleux à toute l'Italie.'[1] This was the most drastic programme. The least drastic was an act of formal homage to France. Hadn't this been the policy of the United Provinces after the terrible war of 1672? 'La république de Hollande, la plus puissante qu'il soit aujourd'huy au monde, s'est bien appliquée à apaiser la colère de Louis et s'est soumise au plus fort.'[2]

Marana was one of the most well-known and widely read journalists and observers of his time (the end of the seventeenth century and the beginning of the eighteenth).[3] He publicized all over Europe the debates I have quoted. Later on, he gave his ideas a new form, comparing them to the tradition of *raison d'état* and accentuating his desire to please Louis XIV. He had already examined with great insight the crisis of 1672 in his *The plot of Raffaello della Torre*, published ten years later in 1682. His *Dialogue between Genoa and Algiers* examined all the struggles caused in Genoa by the bombardment of Duquesne. Shortly afterwards his *The Turkish spy* began to come out volume by volume. He had begun it in Italian for Louis XIV, and had continued it in French. The work was soon translated into several other languages.[4] It was a history of the seventeenth century in epistolary form, interspersed with observations on the usages, customs and constitutions of the world which became increasingly non-conformist both religiously and politically. The literary device of the letters written by a Turk from Europe gained such a hold over Marana that,

[1] Marana, *Dialogue*, p. 128. [2] *Ibid.* p. 134.

[3] There are many important documents regarding him in the State Archives of Genoa, Politicorum, 1659, no. 133, Lettere ministri Francia, 2201, 2201 *bis*, 2202, 2203, 2204.

[4] J. E. Tucker, 'The *Turkish Spy* and its French background' in *Revue de littérature comparée*, 1958, pp. 74 ff.

almost imperceptibly, he passed from the most evident adulation of Louis XIV, from the desire to strengthen his own position, and to praise a great and powerful state which was no longer bound by the exclusive privileges of caste, to a political vision in which diversity was not only tolerated but welcomed as natural and beneficial. The ancient contrast between the republican tradition and the monarchical softens in his pages into an increasingly sceptical and tolerant vision.

Thus, from a comparison between his native Genoa and the France of Louis XIV, Marana had created something which might have attracted the mind of the young Montesquieu. In fact, *L'espion turc*, as is well known, was not only to be a literary incitement to the *Lettres persanes*.[1] Marana had become a *philosophe*. One reads in the preface to an edition of his work which came out at the very beginning of the new century: 'Il raisonne sur les causes des soulèvemens et des bouleversemens des états non en barbare, mais en habile politique et en sage philosophe.'[2]

The situation in Venice was apparently different in the seventeenth and eighteenth centuries. It was only with the peace of Passarowitz that the republic of San Marco retired from the great international conflicts. It never again allowed itself to be dragged into a war, whereas this happened once more to Genoa. Its neutrality in these years was a rather better protection against the passage of armies and their depredations. Yet, substantially, the situations of Venice and Genoa were very similar. Throughout the eighteenth century Austria pursued a systematic policy designed to isolate Venice and rob it of any commercial power. The land routes of Lombardy were to replace those passing through Venice, while Trieste was to replace the republic in the Adriatic. As everyone knows, in the end Vienna conquered Venice, at the end of the eighteenth century and the beginning of the nineteenth, when it was able to take advantage of the upheavals caused by

[1] Ernest Jovy, 'Le précurseur et l'inspirateur direct des *Lettres persanes*' extracted from the *Bulletin du bibliophile*, Paris, 1917, and Montesquieu, *Lettres persanes. Texte établi, avec introduction, bibliographie, notes et relevé de variantes par Paul Vernière*, Paris, 1960, pp. x–xi.

[2] *L'espion dans les cours des princes chrêtiens*, twelfth edition, Cologne, 1700, vol. I, *Préface particulière*, pages unnumbered. Interesting pages on the Italian republics can be found in another writer known and appreciated by Montesquieu, Paolo Mattia Doria, *La vita civile*, Naples, 1710 and other editions. Cf. in the edition of 1753, pp. 236–7.

Napoleon. But for many long years Venice reacted to this slow process of absorption with the typically republican reflex of immobility. It followed a policy of programmatic conservatism. It tried to withdraw from the daily course of events to contemplate itself in its perpetuity. The image of the sixteenth and seventeenth centuries, the image of the Venetian state in perfect equilibrium, a political masterpiece, was overlaid with the concept of an historical right to eternal existence. Yet, from the 1730s on, one finds here and there the realization of how weak the republic was politically, and the nature of this weakness. Scipione Maffei, that great scholar, was able to use his own personal observation of Holland and France to analyse the fundamental weakness of Venice. It lay in the unhappy relationship, consolidated over the centuries, between domineering Venice and the oppressed and exploited cities of the mainland. His *Consiglio politico* of 1737 is one of the first signs of an awakening consciousness of the Venetian crisis.[1] Andrea Tron, one of the most enterprising senators, was also able to draw on personal experience of other countries. He could not but see how precarious a government must be which remains in office for only a few months, where responsibility rotates not in order to secure an efficient government but simply to hold the balance between the families of the ruling class and the ambitions and careers of their offspring.[2] Yet, however critical he may have been of the Venetian system, he thought the case of Holland was worse. The 'great revolution' of 1747 seemed to him to have reduced 'that republic which was in part oligarchic, and in part democratic' to a 'sort of monarchy'.[3] Thus, when he again confronted the problems of his own country, he could advise no other remedy than that of granting privileges to one of the traditional magistracies of the republic, the Council of Ten, which was to be assigned the power and political force which he

[1] Arnaldo Momigliano, 'Gli studi classici di Scipione Maffei' in *Giornale storico della letteratura italiana*, 1956, no. 403, p. 372.

[2] Giovanni Tabacco, *Andrea Tron (1712–1785) e la crisi dell'aristocrazia senatoria a Venezia*, Trieste, 1957.

[3] *Ibid.* p. 68. Cf. what Andrea Tron wrote in 1743 and 1744 on Holland, as he became more and more disillusioned with that country. 'The republic of Holland has not the prestige it once had...Be consoled by the fact that this republic is beyond all comparison governed worse than ours...It is degenerating little by little into anarchy ...' *Venetiaansche Berichten over de Vereenigde Nederlanden van 1660–1795*, edited by P. J. Blok, The Hague, 1909, p. 384.

increasingly felt was necessary. One almost hears the echo of Genoa's claim to base a dictatorship on the state inquisitors. It seemed increasingly obvious to Andrea Tron that what the ancient republics really lacked was the nucleus of a bureaucratic state. Why should we be surprised that when they tried to find something to take its place they should turn to one of those organs which had established themselves in the republics in the age of the seignories, reflecting within the republics an evolution similar to the one taking place at that time in the monarchical states?[1]

One of the most thoughtful and cultured minds in mid-eighteenth century Venice, Marco Foscarini, was also examining the means and the possibilities for the republic's survival.[2] He did so by subtle political and historical analysis. He had been brought up in the cult of 'the most famous republic that ever was'. His experience as ambassador in Austria reconfirmed this conviction. He wrote his *Storia arcana* in 1735 'to uncover the defects of monarchies, which are in danger of perishing through the vices of a few'. Venetian neutrality became for him a sort of moral commandment. It was certainly not the fear of arms which kept his country out of conflict and wars, but an explicit determination not to be involved in the baseness of the world. 'It is in that way that moral perfection not only consists in doing virtuous works, but also in abstaining from bad ones, and that silence well used is sometimes eloquence.' Venice could only return to its past and seek there the reason for its existence. Foscarini is explicit and severe in his condemnation of the political theory of the *raison d'état*, which had been the instrument of absolutism, of monarchy, and, at the same time, of the decadence of both Italy and Venice. One should start again from the Middle Ages. The history and the study of 'the character of the nations' were 'the principal sources of this civil ability to govern republics'. Thus, Foscarini started from ethics and from history, with a movement which took him well beyond the point at

[1] The history of the Genoese state inquisitors still has to be written. They were created on the model of those of Venice. Cf. Vito Vitale, *Breviario della storia di Genova*, vol. I, pp. 286–7. On Venice and the long struggle between the Senate and the Council of Ten see, above all, the excellent book by Gaetano Cozzi, *Il Doge Nicolò Contarini*, Venice–Rome, 1958, and the same scholar's observations made during his course at the Faculty of Political Science of Padua University, *Politica e diritto nella riforma del diritto penale veneto nel Settecento*, Padua, 1966–7, pp. 8 ff.

[2] F. Venturi, *Settecento riformatore*, pp. 277 ff.

which a 'return to principles' of Machiavellian inspiration would have led him. His thought opens out into a freer vision of historical research as an indispensable element to affirm the right of nations to a separate and independent existence. Marco Foscarini could still be attracted in the 1740s by Piedmontese efficiency. He admired the ability of the dukes of that region to transform it from a country 'cast down rather than stimulated by poverty', 'from a little land without a national industry' into a land of 'industrious and frugal men'. But by now the course of action he wished to recommend to Venice was clear to him. Venice should take up its ancient laws once more to reform the existing ones: it should exhume its ancient regulations to correct contemporary errors and defects. To his eyes, the past and history were like an intangible mould into which present exigencies should be cast, almost as if to ensure a sense of legitimacy, as if to consecrate provisions imposed by necessity, by need, by the pressure of everyday life. In 1752, he published his longest work, *Della letteratura veneziana libri otto*. (It deals in fact only with political, historical, juridical and scientific works.) It was not the laws of Rome or the eloquence of Cicero which had ensured the survival of the Venetians through the centuries, but 'their own, proper right', their own language and their own varied and complicated culture, so different from that of other countries. His ideal was Paolo Sarpi, not the humanists, much less the supporters of the *raison d'état*. The model of the republics of the ancient world would not help one to understand Venice, nor would it help Venice to live. The republic of San Marco was different because of its mercantile character. It had been rich and patrician from the outset.

Foscarini lived to become a doge and did much to revive the thought and politics of Paolo Sarpi. A contemporary justly described him as 'patriae libertatis defensor potius quam corrector'. But the enlightened reformers of the second half of the century took their starting point from the myth which he created of the Venetian republic. In some cases, they even remained prisoners of this heartfelt defence of a freedom which had become a custom and 'the character of a nation', rather than a political possibility and struggle.

The situation in Tuscany was less striking but no less significant. Was it possible to return to the Middle Ages to renew political forms in a country in which the grand-ducal state of the sixteenth and seventeenth centuries was crumbling? What would happen after the death of Cosimo III and his children? Could the republics of Florence and Siena rise again if the Medici state ceased to function? This, too, was a dream of the 1720s and the 1730s which, nevertheless, left its trace in the spirits of the Tuscans of those years. When Giangastone, the last of the Medici, died in 1737 the eyes of many turned to the past. They were drawn to the Etruscan world, which had also been republican and federal. Above all, they were drawn to the great age of 'civic humanism' which was being rediscovered and revalued at that very time by learned Florentines such as Lami, Mehus and others. The ancient republican magistracies had lived on as relics in a museum, overshadowed by the prince and the grand duke. Could they come back to life after centuries of inertness? Would the Medici restore those liberties to the cities which they had suppressed in the Renaissance and in the Italian crisis of the sixteenth century? These shades from the past seemed to convince even men such as Muratori and d'Argenson for a moment. Then Tuscany was assigned to the Lorraines and Richecourt began to lay the foundations of those levelling and modernizing reforms which enabled the grand duchy of Pierre Leopold to become from 1765 on one of the most successful models of enlightened despotism in Europe. But, even then, the republican past of Tuscany continued to be a real presence. A large number of the intellectuals remained opposed to Richecourt. It was an opposition which looked back to medieval Florence, and which increasingly sought its model and ideal in English freedom. It found in Montesquieu the definitions for a constitutional order. At the same time it was rediscovering the republican side of Machiavelli. Thus, its constant attack on despotism combined various shades of opinion. The Tuscany of Pierre Leopold was not to be only an admired example of a reforming state. It was also to be the birthplace of the first attempt at constitutional government in Italy; the land in which the search for a new liberty was most amply and variously stimulated, from Antonio Niccolini to Giovanni Ristori and Filippo Buonarroti, by the experience of the republican past.[1]

[1] F. Venturi, *Settecento riformatore*, pp. 299 ff.; Mario Rosa, *Dispotismo e libertà nel Settecento. Interpretazioni repubblicane di Machiavelli*, Bari, 1964 (useful also for the study of the relations between the English representative, John Molesworth, the son of Robert, the well-known commonwealthman, and the Tuscan circles). On the

The last great blaze of this republican and communal tradition, which had been smouldering under the ashes of Italian decay, burst out in Genoa in 1746. The city was threatened by Charles Emanuel III, king of Sardinia. It was occupied and oppressed by the troops of Maria Theresa. It rebelled, chased out the Austrians, and then threw itself into a long and resolute war under its own walls, and in the Ligurian mountains. Thus Genoa succeeded in reconquering its freedom and independence at first alone, and then aided by the French. The treaty of Aix-la-Chapelle confirmed this newly-reconquered liberty. All this is well known. It acquires historical significance only if we see things from within, from inside the Genoese palaces and houses. We are confronted by the last page in the history of an Italian medieval republic. The revolt sprang from the masses. It fed on the contempt and hatred they felt for the nobility who were unable to defend the city. The government, at that time often called 'the Republic', was caught between two fires, the Austrians and the people's revolt. It hesitated and wavered, restricted by its desire to preserve both independence and privileges. The unity of the governing class was destroyed. The poorer nobility demanded greater participation in government. The more ancient nobility struggled with the more recent. Each family group sought its own way out. The laws in 1528 and 1576, which had secured the stability of the republic, were called into question again. An autonomous power was being formed outside the governmental palace. At first it was the general headquarters of the people. Then it became a general assembly, with representatives from the groups of armed men, city areas and corporations, and peasants from the neighbouring villages. It had its own government commissions, to which the officials were elected. There was a grand chancellor of the people. The assembly undertook to report frequently to the whole population gathered in the piazza. The very structure of the aristocracy seemed endangered. Military necessities and the French

discussion about Machiavelli, the most studied part of the history of the republican tradition in Tuscany and elsewhere, cf. F. Raab, *The English face of Machiavelli. A changing interpretation. 1500–1700*, London–Toronto, 1964, and Giuliano Procacci, *Studi sulla fortuna di Machiavelli*, Rome, 1965. On the political problems of Tuscany see Furio Diaz, *Francesco Maria Gianni dalla burocrazia alla politica sotto Pietro Leopoldo di Toscana*, Milan–Naples, 1966. Cf. as well A. Saitta, *Filippo Buonarroti*, Rome, 1960, and Carlo Capra, *Giovanni Ristori da illuminista a funzionario. 1755–1830*, Florence, 1968.

pressure caused the government of the nobles to regain control, however slowly. It was as if Genoa had run through all the centuries of its history in the space of a few months, as if it had lived through the whole process which had gradually made it the most typical and closed of the oligarchical republics once more. Evidently the process could not be reversed. Yet it had been a profound shock and had made a strong impression on many contemporaries. The whole range of the problems of ancient and modern republics was under discussion: the relations between aristocracy and the common people; the limitation of the power of the aristocracy itself within a small oligarchy, coupled with the problems of a direct democracy and the forms which the representation of the people should take; and the very way in which representatives should be elected, removed and constituted. Last but not least, there was discussion of the problem of the relationship between the dominating city and the territories administered by it, whether they were to be found along the Riviera, or on the island of Corsica. The rebellion in Corsica was going on, and the last decades had already shown that the island could not be subdued again.[1]

All these problems were eventually suppressed by the timorous and careful restoration of the status quo by the Genoese nobility. But one has only to open the newspapers, chronicles and histories of those years in Italy and, even more so, in other countries to realize how these questions were widely and animatedly discussed. What struck contemporaries was the lack of a centre of power in the Genoese revolt, and the uncertainty of its development. These phenomena were due to the dispersion of its energies in the many forces which came to the fore in those months—the patrician government, the parishes, the trades and the militias. All these centres were held together only by the determination not to be subjugated by Austria or Piedmont. They were united in defending their ancient liberty, which traditionally and intuitively they identified with independence. In Genoa too the very existence of the republic remained the essential problem in the face of the attack of the absolutist states, the monarchies. The play of internal forces, their organization and political strength, were all eventually subordinated to the primordial necessity of survival. This was noted perhaps most clearly by a modest but curious Genoese

[1] F. Venturi, *Settecento riformatore*, pp. 198 ff.

observer of those years, Francesco Maria Accinelli. He wrote that there had been many Italian republics in the Middle Ages. But then they had been dominated by tyrants and by princes, or 'it had been wiser for them to submit to the arrogance of those who had grown powerful through the usurpation of the states and territories of others'. Only Genoa, 'the most ancient among those surviving, as it was also the most tormented, the most insidiously threatened and oppressed, can boast of having overcome every difficulty and of maintaining its native liberty and honour'. It was more fortunate than the other republics, of Holland, Switzerland, Venice and Lucca. By the middle of the eighteenth century Genoa was safe within its borders. The grip in which it had been tightly held in the previous centuries seemed to slacken after 1748. Accinelli, with an optimism typical of the age, felt sure that Genoa could face the future with a certain tranquillity. There were no longer within its confines 'robber eagles, nor animals intent on getting fat', but 'mild and peaceful princes, each contented with his lot'.[1]

The problem of the republics was at that time at the centre of the debates which were taking place at Pisa university towards the end of the forties. A group of Genoese emigrants and students had gathered round a philosopher, Gualberto de Soria. The results of their discussions were made known in a work entitled *Notti alfee*, today preserved in the Labronica library of Leghorn.[2] The backwardness of the Genoese structures appeared very clearly. There was no economic policy which went beyond the interests of the family groups making up the patriciate of the republic. The Corsican revolt could never be settled without profound changes in the organization of the state. The lack of a cultural policy was just as evident. There was no university and no centre for the discussion of the political and economic problems of the state, nor for the formation of a better governing class.

At Pisa this debate moved on to the enlightened reforms of the second part of the eighteenth century. In the countries beyond the Alps the revolt of Genoa and the events in Holland were also widely commented on and discussed. In France, England, Germany, and above

[1] Francesco Maria Accinelli, *La verità risvegliata, con tre dissertazioni della decadenza dell'Impero, della libertà di Genova, della soggezione di S. Remo alla Repubblica.* MS. preserved at Genoa in the Berio library, ff. 1 and 5.

[2] F. Venturi, *Settecento riformatore*, pp. 349 ff.

all in Holland, curiosity and interest were most intense. The vicissitudes and fortunes of diplomacy and war had led the United Provinces and Genoa to opposite ends of the international alignment; with the Empire against France, and vice versa. But the problems of the two states were not really so dissimilar.

First of all, were they to be neutral or belligerent? The argument was lively and manifold, but the conclusion was unanimous. By the middle of the eighteenth century, the old republics could survive only if they withdrew from the conflicts of the great powers. There were to be no alliances and no wars. Both Holland and Genoa ended by admitting that Venice was right. In the middle of the eighteenth century the commercial state had to be neutral. The example of the classical republics was fatal to them, the worst the modern ones could follow. As one of the pamphlets of the age said: 'L'ambition est le fléau des républiques, la jalousie et les dissensions en sont la perte. Les anciennes républiques ont été détruites par ces passions. Les modernes doivent l'être nécessairement de même.'[1]

There was another fundamental problem. Did the policies of the absolutist states and their desire for conquest make internal change indispensable within the republics? Was a stadtholder necessary in Genoa as well? Might it be that population had fallen once more under the power of the nobility because it hadn't found a leader and so hadn't been drawn towards a dictatorship? The answers to these and similar questions given by contemporaries largely depended on their political affiliations. The supporters of Austria praised the figure of the stadtholder, the supporters of France believed in the rule of the Genoese nobility. But this debate did not wholly depend on a political alignment. For example, a contribution was made by one of the most adventurous writers of the eighteenth century, Ange Goudar. He proved able to understand that the internal rivalries of the classes was the military feature of a non-professional war; a war desired and conducted by a large part of the population.[2] Goudar used the republican

[1] *Le roi de Hollande, ou la République détruite par ses Stadhoulders. Dernière partie de la fin des révolutions*, n.d., n.p., p. 22.

[2] On Ange Goudar, see Joseph J. Spengler, *Économie et population. Les doctrines françaises avant 1800. De Budé à Condorcet*, Paris, 1954, pp. 63 ff., L. S. Gordon, 'Nekotorye itogi izučenija zapreščennoj literatury epochi prosveščenija (Vtoraja polovina XVIII v.)' in *Francuzskij ežegodnik*, 1959, pp. 101 ff.; Francis L. Mars, 'Ange Goudar, cet inconnu' from *Casanova gleanings*, no. 9, Nice, 1966.

model to examine, discuss and criticize the social and political reality of the French monarchy and of the other European states. He certainly used his first-hand knowledge of the Genoese experience in his first important book, *Les intérêts de la France mal entendus*,[1] the starting point of a long adventurous career of an international pamphleteer.

On the international scene, the conclusions were unequivocal as well. The France of Louis XV should now be considered as a power which tended to maintain the status quo in the republics of the Low Countries and of Italy. Within each republic it supported the existing rulers. French foreign policy requested only that the republics should remain unchanged and neutral. 'Les nations frontières de la France' need not worry. The times of Louis XIV, when the conflict between monarchy and republic had had a clear ideological significance, had passed. Now France, 'loin de vouloir troubler le repos des républiques, ni envahir leurs possessions, s'en déclare le ferme appuy'.[2] The absolutist states accepted the survival of the republics, and the latter remained unchanged and neutral. Both political forms seemed to lose some of their ideological importance in that moment of equilibrium which the *ancien régime* appeared to have achieved in the middle of the century. The cycle of wars and conflicts inaugurated by the Sun King was over.

But this equilibrium was neither easy nor lasting. One has only to read the *Mercure historique et politique* to see how contemporaries realized that the peace of Aix-la-Chapelle had been accompanied and followed by a wave of disorders, rebellions and conspiracies. However dissimilar in form and importance they may have been, they all seemed to be directed against the fiscal and financial policies of the states of those times. They opposed the tax farmers, the excise men, the customs officials, and the national debt. From Palermo to Paris, from Genoa to Amsterdam, even to some degree in Spain and Berne, this was the typical crisis of the middle of the century. At this time many states revealed themselves to be too weak and uncertain after the war to continue their task of re-organization and rationalization. La Ensenada in Spain, Machault in France, William IV in the United

[1] Amsterdam, 1756.

[2] *Suite des révolutions Hollandaises ou le rétablissement des rois de Frize*, n.p., 1747, pp. 29–30.

Provinces, were the expression of their times. The more slowly they proceeded with reform, the more grave the discontent they produced. The absolutist governments took refuge in conservatism, which resembled the nobility of the ancient republics. The latter were threatened in Holland, in Berne and in Geneva, but finally succeeded in restoring and maintaining their power once more. Similarly the old structures of privilege, the constituted authorities, the whole framework of the monarchical state, especially in France, was again in a phase of resettlement. The new wave of demands of the parliaments in France dates from the middle of the century. These movements were only assimilated and controlled in those states which succeeded in becoming enlightened despotisms and carrying out reforms. Austria is an example. In Paris the conservatism of the established power began to be opposed by the *Encyclopédie* also, a means of increasingly radical criticism, and the beginning of a new interpretation of ever more widespread unrest and discontent.[1]

Montesquieu's great book had been published in this very time, in 1748. In it we can find the fruit of his long experience of those problems we have been discussing. His supreme capacity for balanced judgments enabled him to give us the formula for the co-existence between republics and monarchies, which was by now established. He lucidly indicated the constitutional evolution the modern monarchy was to face. He also predicted the form and content of the reborn republican myth. Of course this is not the time or place to reopen the discussion of the significance of Montesquieu's thought. The continued vitality of this discussion may be seen in the ease with which it is continuously resumed, studied and interpreted, even with such different methods and from such different points of view as those of Robert Shackleton and Louis Althusser.[2] But of course it is not a general interpretation of Montesquieu which is here in question. I should just like to observe how interesting and illuminating the reading of *Esprit des lois* can be in the light of the discords and

[1] Pieter Geyl, *Revolutiedagen te Amsterdam* (*augustus–september 1748*). *Prins Willem IV en de Doelistenbeweging*, The Hague, 1936; Antonio Matilla Tascón, *La Única contribución y el castasto de La Ensenada*, Madrid, 1947; Furio Diaz, *Filosofia e politica nel Settecento francese*, Turin, 1962; F. Venturi, *Settecento riformatore*, pp. 262 ff.

[2] Robert Shackleton, *Montesquieu. A critical biography*, Oxford, 1961; Louis Althusser, *Montesquieu. La politique et l'histoire*, Paris, 1959.

agreements between monarchies and republics in 1748, the age of Louis XV.

The problems of that time arise from every page: the size of the republics ('il est de la nature d'une république qu'elle n'ait qu'un petit territoire'),[1] the problem of the federal republics, that is, of Holland, Switzerland, and the Germanic Empire, 'qui sont regardées en Europe comme des républiques éternelles',[2] the spirit of the republics, which is one of 'paix et la modération', that is to say: they gave up all ideas of expansion in return for their continued existence. He noted the internal dangers which constantly threatened isolated republican cities ('si une république est petite, elle est détruite par une force étrangère; si elle est grande, elle se détruit par un vice intérieur'),[3] the kind of corruption with which they are always afflicted, as the Italian cities showed clearly to all ('on était libre avec les lois, on veut être libre contre elles...La république est une dépouille'),[4] the constant danger to which these forms of government are exposed of falling into the hands of a very limited group of the nobility, or, on the contrary, of undergoing a revolt of the people and thus ending up under a leader. One reads that when the very principle of a republic is corrupted, the republic 'ne subsiste qu'à l'égard des nobles et entre eux seulement. Elle est dans le corps qui gouverne et l'état despotique est dans le corps qui est gouverné, ce qui fait les deux corps du monde les plus désunis.' (This observation could constitute a rapid and accurate sketch of Genoa at the moment of the revolt.)[5] I could go on in this way, speaking of the 'luxe', commerce, evil laws, etc.

Yet Montesquieu believes that virtue is the principle of a republic, and it is quite certain for him that this form of government is normally superior to the monarchical one, based on honour. Indeed, virtue is morality itself, the 'mœurs', the ability to dictate its own laws and to put them into practice. In the *Esprit des lois* this ideal of a republic reminds one of the world of Greece and Rome. Armed in this way it confronts the modern world like a bright and fascinating apparition. But we should not be deceived by the classical luminescence of this vision of Montesquieu. A closer examination shows that his republic was also modern. It was the model from which the contemporary

[1] *Esprit des lois*, book VIII, chap. XVI.
[2] *Ibid.* book IX, chap. I.
[3] *Ibid.* book IX, chap. I.
[4] *Ibid.* book III, chap. III.
[5] *Ibid.* book VIII, chap. V.

republican states had deviated to such an extent that they had become unrecognizable, but it was still there, and they still had the right to refer to it. These republics, as the ancient ones, were not based on direct and universal democracy but were rather 'républiques de notables'. They were based on the capacity of the people to choose and follow their own representatives.[1] This form of government, 'a besoin, comme les monarques et même plus qu'eux, d'être conduit par un conseil ou sénat'.[2] In short, it is the constituted bodies which count. They make the decisions. It is they who are concerned to prevent a return to despotism, the constant threat to all forms of government, both monarchic and republican. Even among the aristocracies, where the constituted bodies are not elected as in democracies, 'quand les familles régnantes observent les lois, c'est une monarchie qui a plusieurs monarques et qui est très bonne par sa nature'.[3] True corruption and ruin begin when constitutional laws are broken, when the nation turns 'à un état despotique qui a plusieurs despotes'.[4] This was exactly what had happened in the Italian republics. Power had been restricted to a very small number of families. The mainstay of a republic, virtue, had been broken by the emergence of hereditary rights and by extravagance. Thus the governments had fallen more or less deeply (more in Genoa, less in Venice) into the abyss of despotism, that is, into the wilderness of a regime where constituted bodies, rules and laws had been swept away.

Montesquieu's criticism of the republics is even more grave and profound. It is an historical criticism. The equilibrium between councils, senates and the people of the ancient cities had been upset for centuries. Classical democracy had disappeared. The modern republics and aristocracies, such as Holland and Venice, had lost their significance, because their monarchies with several monarchs were an anachronism. The attempt to keep constituted bodies alive without the protection of a monarch had become increasingly difficult. Thus these states had become vulnerable to attacks from outside and to the dwindling in number of the oligarchies, as well as to insurrections by the people. Virtue was still the political ideal *par excellence.* But the historical problem posed by the modern republics could only be

[1] L. Althusser, *Montesquieu*, p. 62.
[2] *Esprit des lois*, book II, chap. II.
[3] *Ibid.* book VIII, chap. V.
[4] *Ibid.* book VIII, chap. V.

solved within the monarchies. It could be solved only within the context of the difficult but fruitful compromise between the structures of the nobility, of the citizens, of the judiciary and the sovereign. This compromise might take the French form, or, undoubtedly better, the English. In the former the constituted bodies became intermediaries. In the second they were the very base of the separation and equilibrium of the three powers. This had been possible in England, but it was not in Venice, because, there, power was in the hands of one group and class.

The decisive conflict in England had taken place a century before. 'Ce fut un assez beau spectacle, dans le siècle passé, de voir les efforts impuissants des Anglois pour établir parmi eux la démocratie. Comme ceux qui avaient part aux affaires n'avaient point de vertu...le gouvernement changeait sans cesse; le peuple étonné cherchait la démocratie et ne la trouvait nulle part. Enfin, après bien des mouvements, des chocs et des secousses, il fallut se reposer dans le gouvernement même qu'on avait proscrit.'[1]

Apart from the irony, which is typical of the Enlightenment, of attributing the failure of the Puritan revolution to the lack of virtue itself, Montesquieu, in this way, reaffirms his conviction that the debate between monarchy and republic had really been decided in England, half way through the seventeenth century. We, too, must turn our attention to England if we wish to understand the significance of the republican tradition in the age in which the Enlightenment was germinating.

[1] *Ibid.* book III, chap. III.

II

ENGLISH COMMONWEALTHMEN

IF ONE THINKS ABOUT IT, the judgment of Montesquieu which I have just quoted on the incapacity of England to establish a democracy in the middle of the seventeenth century, and on the inevitable restoration of the monarchy 'après bien des manœuvres, des chocs, et des secousses', is less negative and disparaging than it might at first appear. It is true that Great Britain had allowed herself to be governed by men who 'n'avaient point de vertu'. The attempts of the British to rid themselves of them had indeed been futile and disordered. But, a century after the Puritan revolution, this judgment seemed rather a detached and impartial historical observation: England, in fact, was too modern to return to the models of antiquity, and too near the modern states to be able to become a republic once more.

Montesquieu's conclusion was shared by all his contemporaries, on both sides of the Channel.[1] On the continent, a conservative equilibrium had been attained between the ancient republics and the monarchical states by the middle of the eighteenth century. In Britain, its equivalent was the compromise, apparently more stable but substantially similar, between the monarchy and the parliament, the cities, the classes and the constituted bodies. If one remembers the great conflicts of the previous century, the problems which engaged London and the provinces in the years immediately after 1748, the naturalization of the Jews or the problem of the National Debt, for example, might well seem ripples on the surface of a great calm sea.[2]

Yet this compromise, this renunciation, as Montesquieu calls it, of democracy and virtue, had been neither rapid nor easy. In Britain also, the republican idea had continued to ferment long after the Restoration of 1660. It had gone on developing, growing and changing, even

[1] Cf., for example, Jean-Bernard Le Blanc, *Lettres d'un François*, The Hague, 1745, vol. II, pp. 349 ff.

[2] Thomas W. Perry, *Public opinion, propaganda and politics in eighteenth-century England. A study in the Jew Bill of 1753*, Cambridge, Mass., 1967; P. G. M. Dickson, *The financial revolution in England. A study in the development of public credit. 1688–1755*. London–New York, 1967.

when it had been relegated to the sidelines of everyday political life. The attempt which Montesquieu had considered ridiculous, had, in fact, continued to generate ideas and hopes, and to give life to groups and organizations. It went on doing so until it had become an essential, fundamental element in the moral and intellectual life of the whole of Europe in the new century. Historical research in these last decades has been particularly aware of the link between the Puritan revolution and the Enlightenment. The books by Zera S. Fink, Caroline Robbins (with Christopher Hill's comment), J. G. A. Pocock, Perez Zagorin, Bernard Bailyn, Hugh Trevor-Roper and J. A. W. Gunn, to name but a few, have shown us the way.[1] Now we can see where this research has led us, thanks to one of the books which constitute the starting point of any discussion of such problems. I refer, of course, to that splendid little book, by J. H. Plumb, *The growth of political stability in England. 1675–1725.*[2] Every page of this essay helps us understand how difficult and even unexpected the attainment of political stability in England in this period was. It clearly shows the forces which started and the forces which opposed this compromise. In the following pages I shall only try to add an ideological note in the margin of Professor Plumb's political and constitutional considerations. In the context of the history of ideas I should like to try to see what survived of the desire for 'democracy and virtue' during the stability achieved in England under Walpole and after.

May I be allowed to say at once that what survived is much more important and vital, at least from the point of view of the history of the Enlightenment, than is often admitted in England. Perhaps it is

[1] Zera S. Fink, *The classical republicans. An essay in the recovery of a pattern of thought in seventeenth-century England*, Evanston, 1945; Caroline Robbins, *The eighteenth-century commonwealthmen. Studies in the transmission, development and circumstance of English liberal thought from the restoration of Charles II until the war with the Thirteen Colonies*, Cambridge, Mass., 1959 (cf. Christopher Hill, 'Republicanism after the Restoration' in *New Left Review*, 1960, 3, pp. 46 ff.); Perez Zagorin, *A history of political thought in the English revolution*, London, 1954; J. G. A. Pocock, *The ancient constitution and feudal law. English historical thought in the seventeenth century*, Cambridge, 1957; Bernard Bailyn, *The ideological origins of the American Revolution*, Cambridge, Mass., 1967; H. R. Trevor-Roper, *Religion, the Reformation and social change and other essays*, London, 1967; J. A. W. Gunn, *Politics and the public interest in the seventeenth century*, London–Toronto, 1969.

[2] London, 1967.

because the history of literature sometimes prevails over the history of ideas; perhaps because the forbidding monument erected by Leslie Stephen almost a century ago to the English thinkers of the eighteenth century has not been entirely removed. There may be other local reasons which escape me. It is certainly true that little detailed and minute research is directed towards this field. Many studies of the most minor figures of the world of the *Encyclopédie* are published in England as well as in the other European countries and in America. They are generally philologically blameless. The most obscure friends and colleagues of Voltaire and Diderot, the whole colourful world of the French *lumières* are studied (and I should certainly be the last to complain). Yet, as far as I know, there is no general study of that extraordinary man, John Toland. Nor has sufficiently thorough research been done on Collins, on Tindal, etc. Deism seems to become interesting only when we come to Bolingbroke, that is, when its political significance changes.[1] Probably the best history of deism is still the one by Gotthard Victor Lechler, published in Stuttgart and Tübingen in 1841.[2]

It really seems that the political stability achieved by England in the first part of the eighteenth century is still so impressive as to prevent any consideration, even today, of those who fought against it, or who wanted to modify it, and who succeeded in transmitting to the new century the message of their opposition and battle.

It is impossible to imagine the Enlightenment in Europe without that message. It is true that all recent studies have tended to see the Puritan revolution in the light of similar, contemporary movements on the continent, in Catalonia, in France and in Naples half way through the seventeenth century. It is true that this broader vision has brought positive results. But it is also true that the English revolution did not cause that surge of ideology on the continent which accompanied all the later European revolutions.[3] The ideas of the Levellers were certainly known but they did not inspire any note-

[1] See, for example, Jeffrey Hart, *Viscount Bolingbroke, tory humanist*, London–Toronto, 1965.

[2] *Geschichte des Englischen Deismus*, Stuttgart–Tübingen, 1841.

[3] Roger Bigelow Merriman, *Six contemporaneous revolutions*, Oxford, 1938; Ernst Heinrich Kossman, *La Fronde*; J. H. Elliot, *The revolt of the Catalans*, Cambridge, 1963; Rosario Villari, *La rivolta antispagnola a Napoli. Le origini* (*1585–1647*), Bari, 1967.

worthy political movements beyond the Channel. The ideas born in England during the Commonwealth were destined to reach the continent only in the philosophical form they received from John Toland and Anthony Collins, i.e. when they appeared as deism, as pantheism, as free-thinking, as an exaltation of English freedom, perhaps even as Freemasonry. It was only in this way that the ideas of the Levellers and of the 'classical republicans' of seventeenth-century England became cosmopolitan and were able to take root in France, Germany and Italy, and act as a powerful stimulus throughout Europe for the burgeoning Enlightenment. For Diderot 'la religion' and 'le gouvernement' were inseparable; the disputes of philosophy and those of politics could not and should not be divided. English deistic thought lay between these two poles, and it was the first ideology originating in England which had a strong influence on the continent.

The problem of the republic may help us find our way through the iabyrinth of rebellions, restorations and revolutions which took place ln the British Isles and later reached the continent. We know how important the ancient models were, together with those of Holland and Venice, for the classical republicans, for Harrington and Neville, for Milton and Sidney. But what interests us here is to see how their heirs and disciples reacted when the hope of a return of the republic became more and more uncertain and difficult, when the compromise of William III became more and more firmly rooted in English soil. The decisive period is the last decade of the seventeenth century and the first years of the eighteenth, let's say, between 1685 and 1715.

Let us consider England from half way through this period, and let us imagine we are looking from the continent, which, I believe, is the only correct perspective from which to see these problems. In the autumn of 1700 Sophia, the electress of Hanover, who had every reason to be concerned by such matters, wondered just how strong were the republican tendencies of those who might soon be the subjects of her family and of herself. The diplomat George Stepney explained to her on 11/21 September of that year that 'les malheurs que les Anglois ont essayé du temps des rois Charles I et Jacques II' would make 'surtout aux étrangers' think that beyond the Channel there was 'un dégoût général contre la monarchie même et que notre penchant naturel pour des nouveautés nous pourroit entraîner aisément à tenter encore s'il y a moyen de former une république sur un fondement si solide que l'ambition d'un seul homme ne soit pas capable de la renverser, comme fit Cromwell'. But Stepney tried to assure the electress. He told her that in spite of their experiences 'le génie des Anglois...n'est nullement porté aux principes républicains...Le souvenir de l'an 1648 nous fait encore horreur.' A republic would mean a civil war. The English knew what this meant and had no intention of beginning again. In any case, the social and political situation of England opposed such a 'république imaginaire'. 'Les seigneurs ne souffriront pas que le peuple leur soit égal, comme en Hollande, et les communs ne se sousmettront jamais à la tyrannie despotique des seigneurs, selon le modèle de Venise. Un mélange de ces deux estats avec un capitaine général pour l'image visible du gouvernement est un projet assez joli sur le papier, mais on le trouvera impossible lorsqu'on le voudroit mettre en practique chez nous.' The English constitutional problem is really well illustrated here by comparing it with the various possible republican models, all of which were clearly present in the minds of Stepney and many others in those years. Nothing would do, neither Holland, nor Venice, nor a variant of the republic suggested by Harrington. The squires were too powerful to accept the rule of the merchants, as in Holland. A Venetian oligarchy was impossible in London. However, these were alternatives reflected in the public opinion of the time, and there were still men in England who discussed them passionately. 'Les esprits inquiets dont notre pays est très fertile s'amusent plus que jamais à feuilleter des libres dangereux qui traittent cette matière, scilicet Sidney *Of Government*, Harrington *Oceana*, dont le dernier est fameux pour avoir esté escrit par un habile homme du temps de la rébellion, et pour être publié d'une belle impression depuis peu par un libertin nommé Tolon comme si la conjoncture présente favorisoit des sentiments semblables', as Stepney added.[1]

[1] *Correspondance de Leibniz avec l'électrice Sophie de Brunswick-Lunebourg*, Hanover n.d., vol. II, p. 209. The Tolon mentioned in this letter is, of course, John Toland, who has left us this impression of the electress Sophy Charlotte: 'L'idée qu'elle a du gouvernement en général est si équitable qu'on l'appelle, dans toute l'Allemagne, *la reine républiquaine*.' John Toland, *Relation des cours de Prusse et de Hanovre*, The Hague, 1706, p. 57.

The restlessness of the 'esprits' had indeed been remarkable in the years immediately before and it would be worth our while to follow it in detail. At that time the club was increasingly taking the place of the drawing-room and even of the tavern in the social life of the country.[1] Discussion of the first principles of government and religion was again widespread, in the provinces as well as in London. Here's an example. Humphrey Prideaux wrote to John Ellis from Norwich on 11 December 1693: 'I find the Republicarians in these parts sedulous to promote atheisme, to which end they spread themselves in coffy-houses and talk violently for it.'[2] In 1697 a senior fellow of Trinity College, Dublin said that these 'persons of miscellaneous education... are secretely forming themselves into clubs and caballs, and have their emissaries into all parts, which are supported by contributions, and I make little doubt that their design is at length to show us that all dominion as well as religion is founded on reason'.[3] In the last decade of the seventeenth century many fundamental texts were written and many published which all tended to unite the republican tradition with radical religious thought. 1694 saw the publication of *An account of Denmark* by Robert Molesworth. In 1696 there appeared *Christianity not mysterious* by Toland. Walter Moyle began his *Essay upon the constitution of the Roman government*. Shaftesbury and John Trenchard, Matthew Tindal and Anthony Collins emerged at this time. A group of men came together who were active in discussion and in the political struggles of the day, on issues ranging from the problem of the standing army to the Protestant succession. They brought to these problems a strong intellectual and emotional commitment, which constantly carried them beyond specific issues to the general problems of religion and freedom. It will be a fascinating task one day to be able to follow their actions, their relationships, their arguments more closely than has been done so far. But what we must note here is that these men saw themselves as philosophers, and not only as politicians or diplomats. They unite and blend, sometimes in a violent and unexpected form, the problems inherited from Spinoza, Locke and

[1] Robert J. Allen, *The clubs of Augustan London*, Cambridge, Mass., 1933, p. 33.

[2] *Letters of Humphrey Prideaux sometime dean of Norwich to John Ellis sometime under-secretary of state, 1674–1722*, edited by Edward Maunde Thompson, London, 1875, p. 162.

[3] Peter Browne, *A letter in answer to a book entitled Christianity not mysterious*, Dublin, 1697, p. 209.

Newton with those which were being debated in parliament and by the makers of foreign policy in England and Europe. This is why they are difficult to define: high and low whigs, old and new whigs, real whigs, republican fringe of the whigs, deists, free-thinkers; all these terms express only a part of the truth. One might consider them, with a slight risk of exaggeration, as the first group of Enlightened intellectuals and philosophers at grips with the political problems of their age.[1]

Seen from this point of view, John Toland is certainly the most significant and characteristic among them. He was capable of the most brilliant intuitions concerning the history of religion, and, at the same time, the most active of those asserting once more the English republican tradition. He was the man who had the greatest and most fruitful relations with the continent, but who never ceased to take an active part in the politics of England in the first years of the eighteenth century. His participation in the struggle over the Protestant succession is of some importance, while he also worked out a materialistic form of Spinoza's philosophy which later, as might be expected, interested Diderot, d'Holbach and Naigeon.

It would be a mistake to divide the political thought of this group into more or less democratic, or more or less aristocratic tendencies. In reality, their reflections and their struggles are interesting because they show us the whole republican tradition, both English and continental, having to face new problems and gradually transforming itself into a new vision of political liberty. In Molesworth we find the Celtic tradition again, the aristocratic opposition, the conviction that freedom is ancient and despotism recent in all Europe. It was he who republished Francis Hotoman's *Franco-Gallia*. It was he who affirmed that 'all Europe was in a manner a free country till very lately'. He studied, with great energy and intelligence, the circumstances which led to the loss of their freedom by the Danes around 1660, and their

[1] Besides the fundamental works cited on page 48, note 1, cf. above all, F. H. Heinemann, 'John Toland and the age of Enlightenment' in *Review of English Studies*, 1944, n. 78; *idem*, 'Toland and Leibniz' in *The Philosophical Review*, 1945, p. 437; Howard William Troyer, *Ned Ward of Grubstreet. A study of sub-literary London in the eighteenth century*, Cambridge, Mass., 1946; Paolo Casini, *L'universo macchina. Origini della filosofia newtoniana*, Bari, 1969; Caroline Robbins (ed.), *Two English republican tracts. Plato redivivus, or a Dialogue concerning government by Henry Neville. An essay upon the constitution of the Roman government by Walter Moyle*, Cambridge, 1969.

fall into the worst kind of despotism.[1] When he considers Italy he, too, is struck by the survival of archaic republican forms. He no longer looks, as Harrington had done, at them as at a model. He doesn't consider them a source of hope, but he believes that one day a new breath of freedom may inspire them, that one day the struggle against the Roman tradition may give life to these political forms as well. 'Italy from several small commonwealths was at length swallowed up by the emperors, popes, kings of Spain, dukes of Florence, and other lesser tyrants. Yet 'tis to be remark'd that the ancient state of Europe is best preserved in Italy even to this day, notwithstanding the encroachments which have been there made on the people's liberties, of which one reason may be that the republicks, which are more in number and quality in that spot of ground than in all Europe besides, keep their ecclesiasticks within their due bounds and make use of that natural wit which Providence, and a happy climate, has given them to curb those who, if they had power, would curb all the world.'[2] But, beyond these remote hopes, Molesworth represents, above all, the continuation and the resumption of internal opposition of the constituted bodies against the centralized and monarchical state. He expresses the English equivalent to the growing opposition in these years in France to the Sun King; an opposition centring upon such men as Boulainvilliers, Vauban and Boisguilbert. This is the comparison which enables us to measure the difference between the situation in England and France. In London, the republican tradition and deism notably modify this aristocratic opposition. Molesworth's violent hatred of despotism and his passionate love of freedom have no parallel in France. He already glimpses the way out of the political contradictions of his age. He sees it in philosophy and in education, and in the struggle against privilege. Thus his political argument is already coloured by an attitude of the Enlightenment. Molesworth concludes on the fate of liberty in Europe: 'Had these countries, whilst they were free, committed the government of their youth to philosophers instead of priests, they had in all probability preserv'd themselves from the

[1] *An account of Denmark as it was in the year 1692*, London, 1694, preface (pages unnumbered); cf. Paul Ries, 'Robert Molesworth's *Account of Denmark*. A study in the art of political publishing and bookselling in England and the continent before 1700' in *Scandinavica*, vol. 7, November 1968, no. 2.

[2] Molesworth, *An account of Denmark*.

yoak of bondage.'[1] Molesworth's contemporaries always considered his thought to be tinged with republicanism. Of course, this did not happen in Paris. In the opinion of one of his opponents, writing in 1694, he was not only a frightening example of the 'depravation of human nature', nor had he only opened 'a school of atheism', exalting 'the venerable name of philosopher above that of priest'. His programme was an 'anti-monarchical project'. His extremism and the passion with which he conducted it against the 'tyranny and arbitrary power' recalled 'the logick of the saints...to uplift the good cause of the days of regeneration'. Molesworth's opponent ended by saying that he was nothing but a 'republican brother', as was shown also by his determination 'to amuse the multitude with much talk about a contract betwixt king and people and drawing wild inferences from it'.[2]

Walter Moyle and John Toland were the foremost among those who revived and invigorated a republican interpretation of antiquity. They went back to the civic humanism of Renaissance Italy, and to Machiavelli. They tried to enlist in their cause the greatest possible number of Latin writers. Above all, they strove to save Livy from the accusation of superstition and of complacency toward Augustus. By so doing they transmitted to the eighteenth century the long tradition which, in the seventeenth, had culminated in Harrington. They tried, in various ways, to re-affirm this long republican tradition before the English people of an age we still call Augustan—further proof of the defeat men such as Toland or Moyle underwent at that time, a defeat which still seems to weigh on them.[3]

Yet their books and pamphlets had considerable influence. Toland and Moyle re-examined problems which their contemporaries found deeply interesting. Why had the popular government of ancient Rome fallen? Because, Moyle explained, it lacked the energy to return to the original forms of government 'by restoring the ancient virtue and discipline', according to the formulas and the ideas of Cicero and Machiavelli.[4] Because a 'mistaken liberty' had allowed exceptions to

[1] Molesworth, *An account of Denmark.*

[2] *The commonwealths man unmasqu'd or a just rebuke to the author of the Account of Denmark*, London, 1694, pp. 2–3, 19–22, 75, 100.

[3] Robbins, *Two English republican tracts*; John Toland, *Adeisidaemon, sive Titus Livius a superstitione vindicatus*, The Hague, 1709.

[4] Robbins, *Two English republican tracts*, p. 253.

the constitution. A forthright dictatorship would have been better than such compromises. 'Nothing can be more certain than that no constitution can subsist where the whole frame of the laws may be shaken or suspended by the sudden temporary councils of the multitude, and where the laws are governed by the people, instead of the people being governed by the laws.' Neither would a sharing of power between the people and the senate have been able to solve the problem, such a power being equally pernicious in whatever hands it was placed.[1] The force of the law had thus been diminished dangerously. This involution had become possible through certain defects in the Roman constitution, by the bad organization of the tribunate and of the censorship, of those institutions which nevertheless were 'of admirable use in maintaining the morals and the virtue of the people'.[2] When the process of decay was under way, even the great men, instead of defending the great fences of their liberties as they had done originally, had thrown themselves against them, and, in a last analysis, had 'destroy'd the commonwealth'.[3]

These were all familiar problems, as we have seen, in the debates on the fate of the republics at the turn of the century, from the relationship between senate, nobles, and people, to the necessity to strengthen one magistracy able to regulate and hold together all the others. Moyle's reflections on the ancient world are thus coloured by the political preoccupations on both sides of the Channel in those years. Many years later this essay by Moyle was published in France. It appeared, in fact, in the year X, or 1801. The translator remarked that one could say about the *Essai sur le gouvernement de Rome* the same thing as d'Alembert had written about Montesquieu's *Considérations sur les causes de la grandeur des Romains et de leur décadence* 'qu'on pouvoit l'appeler l'histoire romaine à l'usage des philosophes et des hommes d'état'. It is curious but noteworthy that he added: 'c'est une chose digne de remarque que les Anglais, cette nation dont les Romains exterminèrent les ancêtres, sont les premiers qui aient écrit des réflexions philosophiques et donné à l'Europe des notions profondes sur l'empire romain. C'est ainsi que les vaincus sont devenus

[1] Robbins, *Two English republican tracts*, p. 255. [2] *Ibid.* p. 258.

[3] *Ibid.* p. 259. In the original edition, *The works of Walter Moyle Esq. none of which were ever before publish'd*, London, 1726, the pages quoted above are in volume I, pages 133, 137, 145, 147, and 148.

les juges des vainqueurs.' He observed that Moyle had been among the first, soon followed by Gibbon, Ferguson, Edward Wortley Montagu and Hooke.[1]

Among all the men in this tradition of thought, John Toland is the one who is closest to the type of the Enlightenment philosopher. His culture was encyclopaedic. His life was free, active and full of enthusiasm. It may seem confused and contradictory, but he was really true to his vocation, which was to live among people and spread his ideas. In John Toland, the republican tradition becomes a way of life, a way of being personally independent, of showing philosophical enthusiasm. He was the poorest of these fellows. He made his living by writing. He distributed unusual manuscripts, organized libraries and literary correspondences.[2] He was also the most cosmopolitan, and the most resolutely opposed to being shut up in the world of pure scholarship. He said that scholars were creatures that he judged 'as useless and contemtible as the worms that help 'em to consume their papers'. He would constantly reaffirm that his inspiration was that of a philosopher and politician, that all his studies were intended 'to render me fit for business and society, especially the service of God and my country'. He wrote this in 1696, in his translation from the Italian of Bernardo Davanzati's treatise on money. He placed Davanzati on the same level as his master, Locke.[3] In the same year Toland revealed what he meant by the service of God and his country with the publication of *Christianity not mysterious*.[4] The title seemed deliberately to mislead the reader. Christianity, in this title, meant what was soon to be known as deism. Original and primitive religion had had no mysteries. However, this was not the case with the pagan and Hebrew religions. Toland's real interest in Christianity as an historical phenomenon was in understanding how and why 'it became mysterious', that is, what process had led it to resemble all the

[1] *Essai sur le gouvernement de Rome. Par Walter Moyle, traduit de l'Anglois. Ouvrage utile aux hommes d'état et aux philosophes*, Paris, an X/1801.

[2] British Museum, Add. MSS. 4295, above all ff. 40 onwards.

[3] *A discourse upon coins by signor Bernardo Davanzati, a gentleman of Florence, being publickly spoken in the Academy there, anno 1588, translated out of the Italian by John Toland*, London, 1696, 'The translator to his friend', March 1695/6, p. v.

[4] *Christianity not mysterious, or a Treatise shewing that there is nothing in the Gospel contrary to reason nor above it and that no Christian doctrine can be properly call'd a mystery*, London, 1696.

other religions of the earth. Why had it yielded to fear and to the deceitfulness of those whom it suited to hide the truth and transform it into mystery?[1] Reason did not allow any mysteries whatever. 'The knowledge of finite creatures is gradually progressive.'[2] The forms of mystery surrounding men were simply the realm of a knowledge which was still to be achieved. Awe and submission before what was not yet known by men was purely and simply superstition and harmful prejudice. One can see that the incipient spirit of the Enlightenment was already strongly visible in the ideas of Toland. It enabled him to understand religions from within, no longer simply as the constructions of an ecclesiastical power, but as an evolution of mysteries and dogmas. It is not surprising to learn that Toland introduced new forms of enquiry into the history of the origins of Christianity, with regard to the Essenes, for example, or the relations between the religions of antiquity, the Mohammedan and the Christian.[3] His book, which could well have been called 'How Christianity became mysterious', also contained an energetic political affirmation. The democratic will which had appeared in the Puritan revolution was raised to a philosophical and religious level. Speaking of the mysteries, he concluded: 'What can seem more strange and wonderful than that the common people will sooner believe what is unintelligible, incomprehensible, and above their reasons than what is easy, plain, and suted to their capacities? But the vulgar are more oblig'd to Christ who had a better opinion of them than these men, for he preach'd his gospel to them in a special manner, and they...understood his instructions better than the mysterious lectures of their priests and scribes.'[4]

His contemporaries already noted that Toland's writings might seem a resumption of the heretical currents of the past, of Socinianism for example. But in fact they represented something new. There was the determination not to admit anything 'contrary to reason or above it',

[1] Toland, *Christianity not mysterious*, p. 168. [2] *Ibid.* p. 75.

[3] On the general problems: Luigi Salvatorelli, 'From Locke to Reitzenstein. The historical investigation of the origins of Christianity' in *The Harvard Theological Review*, 1929, p. 263; the comment of Fausto Parente, 'Il contributo di Luigi Salvatorelli alla storia d'Israele e del cristianesimo antico' in *Rivista storica italiana*, 1966, III, pp. 479 ff. On the eighteenth-century echo of Toland's ideas on the origins of Christianity, cf. F. Venturi, *Saggi sull'Europa illuminista*, I, *Alberto Radicati di Passerano*, Turin, 1954, pp. 236 ff.

[4] Toland, *Christianity not mysterious*, p. 147.

the invitation to consider 'the common people', the aim to achieve a society constructed rationally, including its political aspects. The new deism was to exist in England amid a host of sects and religious currents. It found support and solace in some of them, but it was never completely identified with any of them. It was never to adopt their forms of organization. On the contrary, it sought new ones, as Toland's *Pantheisticon* shows. It never solidified to the point of becoming a formal movement, but remained constantly rationalistic and 'enlightened' in the midst of the very various religious currents inherited from the past.[1] As Toland wrote in his *Clito. A poem on the force of eloquence*, which so scandalized his contemporaries, the determination of deism was to:

> Dispel those clouds that darken human sight
> And bless the world with everlasting light.[2]

Then, almost in the same breath, Toland went on to politics:

> I'll sing the triumph of the good old cause,
> Restore the nation its perfect health,
> The power usurped destroy,
> And form a commonwealth.[3]

Among his many writings directed towards this double yet unified goal, the most successful and effective were probably his biographies and editions of Milton and Harrington in 1698 and 1700. When he spoke of Milton, he laid particular emphasis on his political life and underlined the fact that in his old age the poet no longer belonged to any of the existing religious organizations.[4] One has only to open his edition of Harrington's works to find a perfect graphic representation of his thought:[5] 'I. Tolandus libertati sacravit, MDCC, commercio,

[1] See, for example: J. Hay Colligan, *The Arian movement in England*, Manchester, 1913 (p. 92, relations with deism); Earl Morse Wilbur, *A history of Unitarianism. Socinianism and its antecedents*, Cambridge, Mass., 1947, vol. II (p. 575, relations between Crellius and Matthew Tindal); G. R. Cragg, *From Puritanism to the age of reason. A study of changes in religious thought within the Church of England, 1660–1700*, Cambridge, 1950 (pp. 136 ff., John Toland and the rise of Deism).

[2] *Clito. A poem on the force of eloquence*, London, 1700, p. 6.

[3] *Ibid.* p. 11.

[4] *The early lives of Milton*, edited with introduction and notes by Helen Darbishire, London, 1934, pp. xxviii ff.

[5] *The Oceana of James Harrington and his other works, some whereof are now first published from his own manuscripts. The whole, collected, methodiz'd and review'd, with the exact account of life prefix'd, by John Toland*, London, 1700.

opificio.' Beside this statement we see the portraits of Brutus and of William III, of Moses and of Solon, of Confucius, Lycurgus and Numa. They unite classical antiquity and the new interest in the history of religions, the libertarian deed of Brutus and the egalitarianism of Lycurgus, with the cosmopolitanism of Confucius, and last but not least, with British freedom and property in the reign of William III. The book was dedicated to the lord mayor of London, 'the largest, fairest, richest, and most populous city in the world', the city in the heart of which stood the bank of England, built according to the model of organization suggested by Harrington. This was the city which could be called the 'new Rome in the west'.[1] From London, Toland directed his appeal for freedom to all. The commonwealthmen no longer belonged to a sect or to a conspiracy. They openly preached their ideas to everyone. 'Who can be so notoriously stupid as to wonder that in a free government and under a king that is both the restorer and supporter of the liberty of Europe, I shoud do justice to an author who far outdoes all that were before him in his exquisit knowledge of the politics?'[2] Freely and openly, he intended to persuade everyone that 'Harrington's *Oceana* is...the most perfect form of popular government that ever was'.[3]

During and after the war of the Spanish succession the situation in Europe at last seemed favourable to the diffusion of these ideas outside England. Toland applied himself to the task with notable effectiveness and success. In Austria he attracted the attention of Prince Eugen and the strange diplomat and free-thinker, Georg Wilhelm, baron of Hohendorf.[4] The manuscripts Toland sent them on the Jewish and Mohammedan religions, on the *Origine et la force des préjugés*, on *Deux problèmes historiques, théologiques et politiques*, have been recently found and examined in the National Library in Vienna by a young Italian scholar, Giuseppe Ricuperati, together with the letters Toland himself sent to his powerful patrons and readers. These papers often contain particularly frank and explicit versions of his religious and political thought. At the same time, he tried to

[1] J. Harrington, *Oceana*, pp. i and iv.

[2] *Ibid.* p. viii.

[3] *Ibid.* p. ix. The dedication is dated 30 November 1699.

[4] Max Braubach, *Geschichte und Abenteuer, Gestalten um den Prinzen Eugen*, Munich, 1950, pp. 126 ff.; Giuseppe Ricuperati, 'Libertinismo e deismo a Vienna: Spinoza, Toland e il *Triregno*' in *Rivista storica italiana*, 1967, II, pp. 628 ff.

establish a similar rapport with Germany, with the electress Sophy, and with Leibniz. In short, Toland tried to give an ideological significance to the alliance of the maritime powers with the Empire and with certain German princes against the France of Louis XIV. The first results can be seen in the papers of his contemporaries in Germany. Leibniz would have preferred Toland to have behaved with 'un peu plus de modération', for example, when writing his life of Milton. 'Il a beaucoup d'esprit et même il ne manque pas d'érudition, mais ses sentimens vont trop loin.'[1] The electress Sophia continued to admire this man 'qui hazarde tout et qui ne se soucie point du qu'en dira-t-on'. But she could not help noticing that Toland's reputation was anything but favourable, so unfavourable, in fact, that his return to England might well be risky. 'Celuy qui brusla le tempe d'Éphèse n'a pas eu tant de réputation.'[2]

Leibniz drew his own political conclusion, writing to Burnet of Kemney on 27 February 1702: 'Il me semble qu'a présent les Anglois qui s'imaginent d'y pouvoir établir une république sont extravagans. Tant que le pouvoir de la France, ou plustost de la maison de Bourbon, subsiste dans un estat si transcendant, c'est beaucoup si l'Angleterre se peut sauver d'un gouvernement despotique.'[3] In fact, the war of the Spanish succession made possible the diffusion of the ideas of the English deists, but it also made a return to republican ideas improbable. The danger of Louis XIV's expansionist policy was too great. A monarchical state was indispensable in England as well. Toland became well aware of this when he returned to England. He had to face a violent storm of criticism, accusations and threats from church and state. The accusation that he was 'a great commonwealthman' became more and more insistent. He was charged with being a heretic. But by now the political aspect of the controversy prevailed and this certainly did not displease him. In 1702, he published one of his most vigorous pamphlets, *Vindicius Liberius, or Mr Toland's defence of himself against the late lower House of Convocation and others.* He quoted a phrase of Tillotson's, almost as if he wished to abandon religious disputes, and concentrate all his efforts on the difficult but not unfruitful political struggle: 'Being (I hope) releas'd from that

[1] *Correspondance de Leibniz avec l'électrice Sophie*, vol. II, p. 333.
[2] *Ibid.* p. 378. [3] *Ibid.* p. 333.

irksome and unpleasant work of controversy and wrangling about religion, I shall turn my thoughts to something more agreeable to my temper.' He made no attempt to hide his republican sympathies, although in the end he admitted that there was no other solution for England except the one resulting from the revolution of 1689. He also agreed that the monarchy of William III really did correspond to some of the fundamental principles for which the republicans had always fought. 'I have been, now am, and ever shall be persuaded that all sorts of magistrates are made for and by the people, and not the people for or by the magistrates: that the power of all governors is originally conferr'd by the society, and limited to their safety, wealth, and glory, which makes those governors accountable for their trust and consequently that it is lawfull to resist and punish tyrants of all kinds, be it a single person or a greater number of men.'[1] This did not mean that Toland advocated democracy, which, he thought, always risked being transformed into anarchy. The vicissitudes of the Puritan revolution still weighed heavily on those who, at the beginning of the century, tried to take up the cause again. Disorder and dictatorship, Cromwell and democracy were still considered undesirable elements. Toland declared he had never asserted he favoured democracy, 'which I think to be the worst form of a commonwealth'.[2] Yet he availed himself of the entire republican heritage and tradition. Of course this was internally divided into a democratic and an aristocratic theme. It had assumed both anarchical and oligarchic forms. But the diverse forms of the republican spirit were of only secondary importance. What counted above all was their unfailing opposition to despotism. Democracy might well be 'the worst form of a commonwealth'.[3] It was still 'a thousand times better than any sort of tyranny'. Thus the republic was separated from the historical forms it had taken in the past, and became increasingly an ideal which could exist in a monarchy such as the English one at the beginning of the eighteenth century, just as it could spread on the continent. It became an incitement to liberty beyond the historical circumstances of the past on either side of the Channel. It was the seed of an enlightened utopia. Here again we might say that the political and religious

[1] *Vindicius Liberius*, p. 126.
[2] *Ibid.* p. 128.
[3] *Ibid.*

problems were parallel. Pierre Bayle had said that atheism was better than superstition. What was important was not the distinction between atheism and deism, but the struggle against prejudices.

Politically, the most difficult problem was the compromise this ideal was obliged to accept with the monarchy of William III, and later of Anne and of George I. Did these sovereigns really represent the best of the republics? Many decided they did, both in England and on the continent. Were the commonwealthmen destined to become the extreme wing of a propaganda which tended to glorify English liberty, and the mixed forms of British government, democratic, aristocratic and monarchical at the same time? Toland himself went as far as possible along this path. Already one of his contemporaries, Thomas Wentworth, writing to his brother (18 August 1710) said that in the pamphlet, *The art of governing by parties* the author had had the impudence to call 'this kingdome a commonwealth', but if one thought it over it was less paradoxical than it seemed. 'King, lords, and commons, each a check upon the other, which is to be calculated for the good of the whole, that it may more properly be called a commonwealth than a monarchy.'[1]

The events of the war of the Spanish succession at first seemed to favour a confluence of the monarchical and the republican traditions. It was almost as if William III had supplied that formula which Holland, Venice and Genoa were looking for in vain. But disappointments soon came. Brutus and William III were only able to stay together for a while. Internal arguments within the group of the commonwealthmen became more and more grave and obvious. In 1707 Molesworth wrote to Shaftesbury expressing his serious doubts about all the initiates 'of the Kitcat and the Junto', who were incapable of forming a coherent position in their political ideas, and 'have changed their principles so often upon the score of dominion' to make one doubt whether 'a free nation ought to rely upon them'. What was needed was a greater detachment from the pressure of daily events, and a greater intellectual independence. 'If a scheme could be made of laying the foundation of future happiness on a set who have not yet bowed their knees to Baals of either extreme, 'twould be the best

[1] *The Wentworth Papers. 1705–1739. Selected from the private and family correspondence of Thomas Wentworth, Lord Raby, created in 1711 Earl of Strafford, with a memoir and notes by James Joel Cartwright*, London, 1883, p. 136.

that could happen to Great Britain.'[1] Shaftesbury certainly listened attentively to Molesworth's appeal but he too was more and more inclined to withdraw from political turmoil, to withdraw into himself, into the world of ideas and of virtue. 'Be it weakness or defect in me, it is my temper. My greatest desire is privacy and retirement', as he wrote on 21 July 1701 to Toland when the latter was at Rotterdam. Shaftesbury was keenly aware of the danger of Toland's tumultuous activity. He sensed that Toland's mingling of ideas and political intrigues risked ruining both ideas and intrigues. He saw Toland on the continent among 'the men of greatest worth and on whom the interest of Europe depends'. So much the greater was his responsibility. He reminded Toland that 'the fame and reputation in the Protestant world and amongst the free people where you are known does in a great manner depend on your behaviour'. It was also for political reasons that Toland and Shaftesbury divided and took separate paths in the years immediately following.[2]

Yet it was the international character of Holland at the beginning of the century which had increasingly convinced Toland and his friends how important it was to introduce their republican ideas into the culture, and, above all, into the political life of their time. In Holland they discovered the heritage of Pierre Bayle. For twenty years Bayle had fought for a vision of life which was, in some ways, parallel to his own. The great French exile had also refused to return to the forms of resistance and revolt, to the religious wars in France. He had argued against Jurieu and against every political religious fanaticism of a Calvinistic and Huguenot inspiration. He had even allowed himself to be accused of betrayal by his fellow exiles in order not to disavow his faith in a more modern state of France, which he believed superior to the traditional municipal, corporative and republican forms. His genius had been expended in the attempt to make the idea of toleration the basis of culture and politics of France and the continent. He no longer believed in any Protestant religious revival. It was a difficult position, which perhaps, even today, has not been sufficiently understood, in spite of the great renewal of interest in Bayle's personality. Too much has been done in the attempt to wrest

[1] Public Record Office, 30/24/20/137, letter from London of 18 December, 1707.

[2] F. H. Heineman, 'John Toland and the age of Enlightenment', p. 133.

from him the secret of his innermost religious convictions. This is always a very difficult thing to do, particularly so with a man of Bayle's ability and lucidity. However, it may be that not enough attention has been paid to the significance of his ideas on Louis XIV, on England, Geneva and Holland. I think we should see still more clearly how convinced he was by then that the wars at the end of the seventeenth century and the beginning of the eighteenth would not re-start the cycle of religious conflicts. History was to confirm his belief. The Edict of Nantes remained revoked. The monarchy of Louis XIV did not allow the exiles to return. Holland and Geneva survived, but they no longer guided a religious and political revival. Yet, the death of Louis XIV was enough for the idea of toleration and the burgeoning Enlightenment to find their centre in the very heart of the greatest monarchical state, in Paris and in France.[1]

The participation of Toland and Shaftesbury in this process, which became European after 1715, was fundamental. They fought against the religious fanaticism of the Catholics and of the mountain people of the Cevennes, of the papist theologians and of their Protestant counterparts. They did so with the vigour if not with the lucidity of Bayle. They were able to use the weapons of irony and political passions. But, above all, they were able to present the model of a society which was both powerful and free, of a state which was not tyrannical and yet was efficient. It was certainly very difficult, if not impossible, to export a monarchy which equalled a republic, as Toland wished. Brutus and William III could not have lived together for very long on the continent either. But when this paradox of the commonwealthmen faded away, there remained a resolute desire for liberty which was nourished by the English republican tradition as well as by the impossibility, observed in all Europe, of undoing the work of the monarchies.

It was not only in France that great interest was aroused by the ideas which had thus matured in England at the time of the war of the Spanish succession. They were able to penetrate mainly through deism, pantheism and even freemasonry. We have seen Toland in touch with Prince Eugen and Baron Hohendorff. In 1712 Toland sent the latter not only his latest 'trouvailles' concerning the history

[1] For bibliographical information see Giuseppe Ricuperati, 'Studi recenti su Bayle' in *Rivista storica italiana*, 1968, II, pp. 365 ff.

of Christianity, but the 'formula sive liturgia philosophica', that is, a first version of his *Pantheisticon*.[1] Through Vienna, Toland's thought greatly influenced the ideas of Pietro Giannone, who had emigrated there after 1723. In his *Triregno*, and later while in prison in Turin, he continued thinking of *Nazarenus* and of what Toland had suggested to him about Titus Livius, Roman history, and the relations between politics and religion.[2] Deism and the Anglo-Dutch culture of the early eighteenth century penetrated deeply into southern Italy in the age of Antonio Genovesi and Raimondo di Sangro, around the middle of the century. They had come through Giannone and the other Italian champions of the state in the struggle against the Curia. After all the name of Toland was by no means forgotten.[3]

To assess the influence of these ideas in Germany, one has only to open the two great collections by Trinius and by Urban Gottlob Thorschmid, the *Freydenker-Lexikon* and the *Freydenker-Bibliothek*, to see the significance of the English deist for German culture. It ranges from the new schools of religious culture of Göttingen to the starting of the *Pantheismusstreit*, more or less coloured with the teachings of Spinoza, from the great influence of Shaftesbury to the success of the nascent masonry.[4] It is certainly true that, as always in the German Enlightenment, the moral and aesthetic temptations made the call for political freedom of the British thinkers less active. The history of this process has still to be written. However, the importance assumed by the commonwealthmen in Germany also in the early eighteenth century is evident.

The process by which Holland became the centre, the workshop for ideas, in the battle against fanaticism is well known. Translations, magazines, visits or lengthy stays by men from England or the rest of the continent made the United Provinces the centre of philosophical and scientific culture in the age immediately after Locke and Newton.

In France the very abundance of examples of the infiltration of deism and free thought after the death of the Sun King makes it

[1] British Museum, Add. MSS. 4295, f. 19, copy of a letter from Toland to Hohendorff, dated 7 March 1711/12, in Latin.

[2] Sergio Bertelli, *Giannoniana. Autografi, manoscritti e documenti della fortuna di Pietro Giannone*, Milan–Naples, 1968.

[3] F. Venturi, *Settecento riformatore*, pp. 523 ff.

[4] Johann Anton Trinius, *Freydenker-Lexicon*, Leipzig and Bernburg, 1759 (photostat edition, Turin, 1960, index); Urban Gottlob Thorschmid, *Vollständige Engelländische Freydenker-Bibliothek*, Cassel, 1766, vol. III, pp. i ff.

impossible for me to give a general picture here. Let's look at one example only. In 1722, maréchal d'Estrées, 'grand d'Espagne, président du conseil de la marine', showed curiosity in the *Pantheisticon* by Toland. When he at last got hold of a copy, he thanked Desmaisaux, through his librarian, Camusat, for 'un si beau présent', and wanted to know about the life and works of Toland.[1] 'M. le maréchal d'Estrée aime beaucoup à connoître les gens de lettres et surtout ceux qui ont pensé aussi singulièrement que les déistes anglois. Nous souhaiterons avoir un recueil de tous ses ouvrages.'[2] He added later: 'les idées de M. Toland sont si extraordinaires que je crois qu'on ne sauroit ramasser avec trop de soins tout ce qui est sorti de sa plume...'[3] This is a single but lively and curious example of the strength of penetration of English ideas beyond the Channel. The greater examples are well known to everyone, from Voltaire to Montesquieu.

To conclude this rather rapid survey of Europe on the verge of the Enlightenment, I hope I may be permitted to recall the Piedmontese nobleman, Alberto Radicati di Passerano. He absorbed the more violent and polemical elements from English deism. He dreamed of a world without property or authority, and, at the same time, showed enthusiasm for the mixed government of the British Isles, which he experienced during his difficult and troubled exile. He combined the most diverse elements from the commonwealthmen in a curious and original way. This becomes all the more interesting if one considers that he came from the most absolutist of the Italian states, and the one most closely linked in its foreign policy with England. You will recall that Robert Molesworth's son was the British representative at the court of Turin at the same time as Radicati was preparing for his religious and political rebellion and his subsequent exile. Every aspect of this example, both the ideological and the political, reveals particularly well the penetration on the continent of the ideas formed in England at the turn of the century.[4]

Let us take a last look at London before turning our attention to the continent, and taking up once more the threads of republican thought and eighteenth-century ideas. It was a decisive moment.

[1] D'Estrées, *Letters*, British Museum, Add. MSS. 4282, letter dated 17 March 1722.

[2] *Ibid.* letter dated 21 August 1722.

[3] *Ibid.* letter dated 21 August 1722.

[4] F. Venturi, *Saggi sull'Europa illuminista*, I, *Alberto Radicati di Passerano*, Turin, 1954.

Queen Anne had died, and the new dynasty was beginning. Our guide will be the curious preface to the French translation of the *Remarks on a late discourse of freethinking* by the famous critic, philologist and historian, Richard Bentley.[1] The French writer in 1738 can look at events with a certain detachment. He observes the document of the birth of free thought, the publication of the book by Anthony Collins in 1713, with an historian's eye. 'Le parlement étoit assemblé. La capitale regorgeoit de monde. Les esprits étoient dans une fermentation terrible. Les *Whigs* craignoient tout pour les libertés et pour la religion du royaume. Les *Toris* ne négligeoient pas le moindre occasion de mettre le pied sur la gorge de leurs adversaires...*Le Discours sur la liberté de penser* venant de paroître dans cette conjoncture critique...'[2] It was attributed to Toland: 'le bruit en courut même fort loin et dura long tems dans les pays étrangers', as may also be seen from the 'Acta eruditorum' of Leipzig.[3] Only later was Anthony Collins recognized as the true author. A veritable political storm burst out against him; he was caught between the prudence imposed on the Whigs and the provocative intentions of the Tories. A keen discussion followed which involved both politicians and scholars, the Dutch and the Germans, as well as the English. When, at last, it was over, Trinius counted at least sixty works directed against him, or produced to discuss his ideas.[4] At first, Collins had to abandon England and flee to The Hague, where he became increasingly associated with the publishers and writers gathered around Leclerc, the heir to the works and ideas of Pierre Bayle. There he collaborated on the translation of his work, *Discours sur la liberté de penser*. 'Ce fut principalement par le moyen de cette traduction que la connoissance d'un ouvrage si pernicieux s'étendit jusqu'aux étrangers.'[5] As one can see, all the elements of the drama were still present in the last act—the close connection between the political struggle and the birth of free thought, the new link which was being established between England

[1] *La friponnerie laïque des prêtendus esprits-forts d'Angleterre, ou remarques de Philéleuthère de Leipsick* [i.e. Richard Bentley] *sur le Discours de la liberté de penser, traduites de l'Anglois sur la septième édition par Mr N. N.* [i.e. A. Boisbeleau de la Chapelle], Amsterdam, 1738.

[2] *Ibid.* preface, pp. v–vi.

[3] *La friponnerie laïque*, p. vii.

[4] Johann Anton Trinius, *Freydenker-Lexikon*, cf. pp. 479 ff. (pp. 120 ff. of the reprint), p. 592 (p. 148 of the reprint), and p. 775 (p. 196 of the reprint).

[5] *La friponnerie laïque*, preface p. xxix.

and the continent in this passage from the republican tradition to the birth of the Enlightenment.

Then the age of political stability began in England. Traditionally it still bears the name which reveals its distant origins. Professor Plumb has called the last chapter of his recent book 'The triumph of the Venetian oligarchy'.[1] It is a revealing title, but some doubts still remain. It is true that Venice was still spoken of in England after 1714, above all on the occasion of the law regarding the House of Lords in 1719.[2] But, in fact, there was less and less discussion of the ancient republics, and the myth of Venice faded as the century progressed. No one could believe any longer that the governing class in the age of Walpole really had anything in common with the Venetian oligarchy. The English compromise was extraordinarily freer and more open, both from the point of view of the variety and mobility of the social forces, and of political liberty. Why then 'Venetian oligarchy'? The term began to be commonly used in the age of Disraeli, as is known. It was not without an element of nostalgia, and even of snobbishness. Thus, 'Disraeli, he who saw the Whigs as having created in the eighteenth century a "Venetian oligarchy" was himself strangely attracted by Venice. He liked to cherish the idea that he was descended from Venetian ancestors, he wrote a novel, *Contarini Fleming*, with a hero supposed to be descended from one of the first of Venetian houses, and it was in Venice, as one of his biographers has said, that he "received the vision of a maritime and trading empire bathed in romantic splendour". It seems likely also that his ideas on the position of the queen were not uninfluenced by the example of the Venetian doge.'[3] It was Harrington become conservative. It is a shadow from the past which still lies over eighteenth-century England, and risks obscuring the more vigorous and new elements. From the point of view of the republican tradition, we should not look towards the oligarchical rigidity of Venice, but towards the harsh struggle which the commonwealthmen, the deists and the free-thinkers were spreading in Holland, in Germany, in France and in Italy. The most lively part of the republican heritage was not the aristocratic element, but the libertarian, as soon became clear.

[1] J. H. Plumb, *The growth of political stability*, pp. 159 ff.

[2] John F. Naylor, *The British aristocracy and the Peerage Bill of 1719*, Oxford, 1969.

[3] Zera S. Fink, *The classical republicans. An essay in the recovery of a pattern of thought in seventeenth-century England*, Evanston, 1945, p. 183.

III

FROM MONTESQUIEU TO THE REVOLUTION

By the middle of the eighteenth century not only did the ancient republics occupy a position of marginal importance compared with the absolutist states, but they were also on the fringe of history itself. Their political importance decreased, while economically the former centres of a flourishing commercial and manufacturing life entered a phase of irreversible decline, the rate and gravity of which varied according to whether it was taking place in Holland or Genoa, Venice or Lucca. The archaic republics survived, but became increasingly distant from the vital centres of Europe, from the centres of convergence and opposition of economic and military forces. Sometimes they lived, like Venice, in a limbo of memories and traditions, convinced of their own continuity and perpetuity. The more their activity decreased, the more they abandoned themselves to the conviction that they existed outside and beyond the hard contingencies which caused strife and internal transformation in other European states.

Ideologically too, the republican ideas seemed to have lost their hold on a political level. They no longer offered an alternative to the ideas and practice of an absolutism which was then beginning to take on the characteristics of the nascent Enlightenment.[1] Neither on the political nor on the theoretical plane, did they seem able to compete with the system then prevailing of natural law. Yet even republican ideas survived. They continued to count in the sphere of morality and customs if not politically. They were outside the active and immediate world of events, outside the conflicts and the battles, but still able to arouse a resolute desire for independence and virtue which, as Montesquieu authoritatively explained in 1748, the monarchical states were not able to satisfy. In the middle of the century the

[1] 'La république d'Angleterre se cache derrière le trône, la Hollande a eu besoin d'un stathouder. Quoique le doge à Venise ne gouverne pas l'état, on lui a donné le nom de prince', said Ange Goudar, in his pamphlet *Naples, ce qu'il faut faire pour rendre ce royaume florissant*, Amsterdam, 1771, p. 11.

word 'republic' found an echo in the minds of many people, but as a form of life, not as a political force. One could conduct an enquiry into the meaning of the word at this time, ranging over books and journals, evocations of the past and the seeds of re-awakening utopias. Admiration and caricature alternated in these images of a republic, industrious and proud, solemn and free. Certainly a republican morale existed when the forms of state organization which had embodied it seemed antique and decaying ruins. There survived a republican friendship, a republican sense of duty, a republican pride, even though the world had changed. These may even have existed in the very heart of a monarchical state, in the innermost self of those who seemed fully integrated in the world of absolutism. It is this ethical aspect of the republican tradition which appealed to the writers of the Enlightenment, to Voltaire, Diderot, d'Alembert, and, of course, to Rousseau. It mingled with the new vision of life being formed in mid-century Paris among the creators of the *Encyclopédie*, on a moral not a political level.

The inspiration came from England. The writer who made the greatest contribution to the transmission of the ethics of the commonwealthmen was probably Shaftesbury. He had been one of the first to withdraw from the political struggle. Freed from the pressure of events, he had raised on to a philosophical plane those ideas which had inspired his friends, Toland, Trenchard, Molesworth, etc. This was the value of his *Characteristicks*. His deistic argumentation against any form of revealed religion had been less harsh, but no less energetic than that of his friends. It had led him to observe with curiosity, mixed with disgust, the traditional forms of religious enthusiasm, or fanaticism. To this he opposed a new enthusiasm which he called social. This constituted the ethical drive of an entirely worldly society, and was wholly directed to bringing about happiness among men. His friendship is very different from the traditional one, and aims at introducing a natural relationship in the context of society. We are not misled by the classical form, in this case as in many others, nor by the recollection of Cassius, or Brutus, or Epaminondas, or Pelopidas. The context of this friendship is different and new. It lies beyond laws and religion, and has its roots in a reality in which states, wealth and ceremony have no part. Shaftesbury's patriotism is equally characteristic. It, too, is entirely optional and, in some ways, alien to the Christian. It is explicitly different from charity, and is also opposed to that instinctive sense of love and attachment to one's native land. This was a passion of 'narrow minds', 'of a mere fungus or common excrescence to its parent-mould or nursing dunghill'.[1] The new patriotism is cosmopolitan and indissolubly linked with freedom. It cannot be conceived, or at least would be absurd, without it. It cannot be felt except by those 'who have really a country and are the number of those who may be called a people, as enjoying the happiness of a real constitution and policy by which they are free and independent'. All kinds of absolute power deny and destroy the very base of true love of one's country. 'Absolute power annuls the publick, and where there is no publick, or constitution, there is in reality no mother country or nation...A multitude held together by force, tho' under one and the same head, is not properly united, nor does such a body make a people. 'Tis the social league, confederacy and mutual consent, founded in some common good or interest which joins the members of a community, and makes a people one.'[2] As we see, the word patriotism itself conveys, in terms of enthusiasm, passion and ethics, exactly the sense of equality and freedom of those who considered themselves the people and the nation in the ancient republics. It was no longer a question of discussing, in political and constitutional terms, where sovereignty lay and how far it extended, nor how it should be constituted. One should feel and revive that sense of independence, liberty and equality which patriotism had stimulated. The new patriotism has a long and rich tradition and it presents itself in a way which all men can and must understand. It is universally human and cosmopolitan.

We are led to similar conclusions by an examination of Shaftesbury's idea of heroism, that is, the complete and immediate identification of the individual with the community. Heroism and philanthropy came more and more to mean the same thing. In danger or in war, friendship involves sacrifice. Yet, as Shaftesbury immediately noted, very little is needed to transform this friend of humanity into a bigot. The

[1] *Miscellaneous reflections. Miscellany III*, chap. I, para. 13. We have used the edition of the *Characteristicks*, n.p., 1745, vol. III, p. 131. Shortly after, in paragraph 20, page 135, he argues against 'the patriots of the soil'.

[2] *Ibid.* para. 12, p. 129.

liberator can suddenly become the oppressor and the destroyer. The new enthusiasm can slip back into the old. This had been another lesson of the Puritan revolution for the men who were about to enter a new century.[1] Thus, Shaftesbury spread his ideas on patriotism, friendship and heroism mingled with an element of irony, of criticism and of objective reasoning. Shaftesbury himself concluded by summing up these various forms in a single enthusiasm for virtue, whose classical and Platonic forms should not be allowed to disguise its modern moral and political content.

In 1745, Diderot published his *Principes de la philosophie morale ou essai de* M. S.*** [Shaftesbury] *sur le mérite et la vertu*. In doing so, he rediscovered the English deist who had been half forgotten on the continent after his rapid rise to fame at the beginning of the century. He also established one of the most solid and lasting bridges between British free thought and French encyclopaedism. This was already clear a year later, in 1746, when his *Pensées philosophiques* appeared. They might be described as comments in the margins of the English writer, and are a vigorous appeal to the passions to liberate man from everything which oppresses him. Thus began that outpouring of writings by Diderot and by his friends, which was to culminate, less than ten years later, in the *Discours sur l'origine et les fondemens de l'inégalité parmi les hommes* by Jean-Jacques Rousseau.[2]

The existence of a republican ferment in France between 1745 and 1754 is confirmed by the diaries of one of the most lucid and independent witnesses of that age, the marquis d'Argenson.[3] France was not spared from that restlessness which spread throughout Europe at the end of the war of the Austrian succession. We have already noted it in connection with the insurrection of Genoa. Neither did it simply reopen and intensify the conflicts between the monarchy and the constituted bodies on the well-known occasion of the attempts at fiscal reform by Machault d'Arnouville. It also assumed a form, which was both more vague and more penetrating, of discontent and

[1] See especially, *An essay on the freedom of wit and humour* in *Characteristiks*, vol. I, pp. 101 ff.

[2] *Discours sur l'origine et les fondemens de l'inégalité parmi les hommes* in *Œuvres complètes publiées par Bernard Gagnebin et Marcel Raymond*, III, *Du contrat social. Écrits politiques*, Paris, 1964.

[3] *Journal et mémoires du marquis d'Argenson*, Paris, 1859 ff.

rebellion. When the marquis d'Argenson tried to describe it, he found himself obliged to call it 'republican'. By December 1747, he was already wondering 'que deviendra la France pauvre et déserte?... Considérons que nos peuples sont aujourd'hui peu attachés à leurs princes...' Thus a possibility, a new virtuality, was disclosing to the astonished eyes of those who closely observed French society: 'Quelqu'un osera-t-il proposer d'avancer quelques pas vers le gouvernement républicain?' His answer, however, was still negative. 'Je n'y vois aucune aptitude dans les peuples; la noblesse, les seigneurs, les tribunaux accoutumés à la servitude n'y ont jamais tourné leurs pensées, et leur esprit en est fort éloigné; cependant ces idées viennent et l'habitude chemine promptement chez les Français.'[1] Five years later, in June 1752, he was already observing how such opinions were evolving 'par le voisinage de l'Angleterre'. 'Le despotisme augmentera-t-il ou diminuera-t-il en France?' He said it would not grow and declared himself convinced that the country was progressing towards liberty 'et même le républicanisme'. 'J'ai vu de mes jours diminuer le respect et l'amour du peuple pour la royauté.' Louis XV had not known how to be a tyrant, nor how to be a 'bon chef de république'. 'Quand on ne prend ni l'un ni l'autre rôle, malheur à l'autorité royale.'[2] In September of the same year, he said he was now convinced that, after the failure of all the attempts at reform of that period, 'la mauvaise issue de notre gouvernement monarchique absolu achève de persuader en France, et par toute l'Europe, que c'est la plus mauvaise de toutes les espèces de gouvernement. Je n'entends que philosophes dire, comme persuadés, que l'anarchie même lui est préférable...'[3]

D'Argenson knew his country and Europe well. Among other things, he had given an overall picture of the different governments of France and of the other European countries in his *Considérations sur le gouvernement ancien et présent de la France*. This work also remained in manuscript. Like his diaries, it was the secret document of a reappraisal which was becoming more and more profound among the ruling class.[4] D'Argenson felt a great admiration for the public spirit which the republics had been able to create and maintain. He had

[1] *Journal et mémoires du marquis d'Argenson*, vol. v, p. 142.

[2] *Ibid.* vol. VII, p. 242. [3] *Ibid.* p. 294.

[4] We have used the edition of Yverdon, 1764.

observed their superior economic enterprise, whether private or by the state. He judged that the circumstances of self-government which created their prosperity could and should be transplanted, even to the territories of the absolutist states, until France achieved a form of democratic monarchy. The king should assume the title Cromwell had usurped, that of protector of the country, transforming the state into a sort of republic protected by the king. As he said in the discourse he applied to the Academy of Dijon for the same prize which Rousseau won with his famous discourse on inequality: 'Les pays d'état et les corps municipaux sont dans la monarchie des espèces de républiques protégées.' Their relations with the monarch should be those of every well-constituted society, 'la liberté et l'égalité'. Intellectual freedom was indispensable while equality was politically even more important. 'Que les législateurs adoptent donc le principe de l'égalité et la terre changera de face.'[1]

But in mid-century, which forces could guide the country along such a road? D'Argenson indicated two: the parliaments and the philosophers. In fact, both were to lead all the movements of the following decades. The constituted bodies and the new forces of the intelligentsia contested the leadership of the opposition, the former from within the monarchical structure itself; the latter becoming even more strongly antagonistic from without. Once again the constituted bodies were to appeal to the ancient constitution of the realm, to a more or less mythical, legal constitution, while the intelligentsia sought its justification with greater intensity in the new ideas of the Enlightenment. In 1751, the first volume of the *Encyclopédie* already contained the manifesto of these new political ideas, Diderot's article, *Autorité politique*. It is not surprising to learn that it was read and used both by members of the opposition of the parliaments, and by the makers of the new 'enlightened' public opinion, which was beginning to play a part in society. Diderot made a great concession to the monarchy, but he concluded, evidently following English models, by affirming that 'la couronne, le gouvernement et l'autorité publique sont des biens dont le corps de la nation est propriétaire, et dont les princes sont les usufruitiers, les ministres et les dépositaires . . . partout la

[1] Roger Tisserand, *Les concurrents de J. J. Rousseau à l'Académie de Dijon pour le prix de 1754*, Paris, 1936, p. 133.

nation est en droit de maintenir, envers et contre tous, le contrat qu'elle fait; aucune puissance ne peut le changer et, quand il n'a plus lieu, elle rentre dans le droit et dans la pleine liberté d'en passer un nouveau avec qui et comme il lui plait...'[1]

A few years later, in 1754, Jean-Jacques Rousseau produced his *Discours sur l'origine et fondemens de l'inégalité parmi les hommes.* In it, he gave birth to a new relationship between the new ideas and the republican tradition. He seemed to have found his lost homeland again. He turned towards Geneva, whose prodigal son he was, publicly and ostentatiously linking himself with the city's long past, just before expanding the radical conclusions his political thought had then reached. His 'enthousiasme républicain' led him to accept not just one or two aspects of his city's past, but the entire heritage, including that patrician aristocracy, those 'magnifiques, très honorés et souverains seigneurs', who governed it. Jean-Jacques states himself a 'citoyen de Genève', and even adds at once, 'citoyen vertueux'. He declared he belonged to a class without political power, but nonetheless patriotic. He had not been born in Geneva, he elected to live there: 'Si j'avois eu à choisir le lieu de ma naissance...' What moved him was not love of his land, but an enthusiasm for an 'état où tous les particuliers se connoissent entre eux...Cette douce habitude de se voir et de se connoître fait de l'amour de la patrie l'amour des citoyens plutôt que celui de la terre.' He was looking for a country in which civil society and government would be indistinguishable from one another and in which the governed and the governors were the same, in which 'le peuple et le souverain soient une même personne'. It was to be a 'gouvernement démocratique sagement tempéré', in which the law ruled and not the political desires of the individual governors, in which tradition was everything and the individual was nothing. You were born and lived a republican, you could not become one. 'J'aurais donc cherché pour ma patrie une heureuse et tranquille république dont l'ancienneté se perdit en quelque sorte dans la nuit des temps.' This was the only way in which a republic could shun all temptation to expand and to conquer, to change its boundaries or to risk internal dissensions between the

[1] *Encyclopédie*, vol. I, 1751, p. 899. Cf. F. Venturi, *Le origini dell'Enciclopedia*, Turin, 1963, pp. 136 ff.

people and the governors, dissensions between 'la vertu des magistrats' and 'la sagesse du peuple', 'marquées par des témoignages de modération, d'estime réciproque et d'un commun respect pour les lois, présages et garants d'une réconciliation sincère et perpétuelle'. So continued for page after page what a contemporary Genevan called 'l'inestimable épître' by Rousseau.[1] It was in reality one of the most curious and paradoxical pieces of evidence of the determination to insert the republican tradition into the heart of the political thought of the Enlightenment itself. It was certainly a difficult encounter. 'L'ancien premier syndic', Du Pan, at once let him know officially. 'Je crains que l'on trouve que vous nous flattez trop; vous nous représentez tels que nous devrions être et non tels que nous sommes.'[2]

Jean-Jacques concluded that Geneva accepted his eulogy politely but coldly. He was never to see again the country which he had wanted to rediscover at the height of its republican enthusiasm. Formey, another contemporary, noted that Rousseau had turned his gaze towards Geneva, but had really seen a utopia.[3] But one of the springs of Rousseau's political thought lay in this very contrast between reality and vision, in this desire to see the ideal republic in the survival of the archaic Genevan constitution. It was this which helped to formulate both his *Du contrat social* and the *Considérations sur le gouvernement de Pologne*. As he himself had said, it was impossible to revive republican forms and sentiments in a country which had yielded to absolutism. In France any attempt to do so was bound to appear paradoxical. But this was exactly what men such as Diderot were trying to do half way through the century. Was it possible for a corrupt people to return to virtue? Rousseau said it was not, and went on to present as an ideal model, capable of inspiring hope, a fossil he had found under the strata of absolutism and which still seemed to preserve the imprint of a fairer and freer state. In theory, it was just as impossible to re-acquire virtue, as it was to return to the state of nature. But there was an example close by, familiar to all, on the very borders of France, which could prove that the republican ideal had not disappeared; that the political will of monarchs and conquerors was not uncontested, that there still existed an alternative possibility.

[1] *Discours sur l'origine et les fondemens de l'inégalité parmi les hommes*, pp. 111 ff.

[2] The definition, by Jacques-François De Luc, is of 20 January 1755, and is quoted in the comment by Jean Starobinski, *ibid.* p. 1286.

[3] *Ibid.* p. 1288.

'Puisse durer toujours, pour le bonheur de ces citoyens et l'exemple des peuples, une république si sagement et si heureusement constituée ...que l'équité, la modération, la plus respectueuse fermeté continuent de régler toutes vos démarches et de montrer en vous à tout l'univers l'exemple d'un peuple fier et modeste, aussi jaloux de sa gloire que de sa liberté.'[1]

If we wish to understand the meaning of this appeal of Rousseau's, we must again turn our attention to the internal relations within the group of *philosophes.* This handful of free and equal men were living through their most tumultuous and fruitful days. The crisis of 1752 was over. The work on the great dictionary had been resumed. They were defended by d'Alembert against external threats from powerful men, patrons, the social and political powers. They were inspired by Diderot. As a guide to understanding this group, let us follow the fate of a young provincial who had arrived in Paris from his native Garonne.[2] He had with him a letter of recommendation from his great fellow countryman, Montesquieu. He had undergone a religious crisis which had transformed him from being intensely devout to becoming passionately eager to absorb the thought of the *philosophes.* At the age of twenty-two, Alexandre Deleyre arrived 'dans cette ville composée à la fois de la lie et de l'élite de toutes les autres...où la foule même repousse l'inconnu dans une effrayante solitude...Le dégoût, l'ennui, la mélancolie attendent à Paris le provincial sans fortune.'[3] His feeling of repugnance for the city, his fear and contempt for the corruption which surrounded him made him turn towards the group of *philosophes* as if towards an ideal city, the only world in which it was possible to live. There he met Rousseau, 'lorsqu'il travaillait à son discours sur l'origine de l'inégalité parmi les hommes'. He saw him, 'plongé dans la plus profonde tristesse se détourner un moment vers son épinette, y préluder ou tâtonner quelques airs pathétiques, couvrir son instrument de larmes et le quitter, soulagé de l'abattement de son âme'.[4] It was Rousseau who introduced him to

[1] *Discours sur l'origine et les fondemens de l'inégalité parmi les hommes*, pp. 116–17.

[2] F. Venturi, 'Un enciclopedista: Alexandre Deleyre' in *Rivista storica italiana*, 1965, no. IV, pp. 791 ff.

[3] Alexandre Deleyre, *Éloge de M. Roux, docteur-régent et professeur de chymie à la Faculté de Paris*, Amsterdam, 1777, pp. 12 ff.

[4] *Idées sur l'éducation nationale, par Alexandre Deleyre, député du départment de la Gironde*, Paris (Convention Nationale), n.d., p. 9.

Diderot. Diderot published two articles by him in the *Encyclopédie*. They could not be more characteristic: *Épingle* which probably provided Adam Smith with the most famous example of his description of the division of work, and *Fanatisme*, an impassioned appeal to the sentiments against religion, developing the opposition of Shaftesbury and Diderot to all forms of institutionalized morality. 'Toi qui veux le bien de tous les hommes...répands l'esprit d'humanité sur la terre...' Deleyre set religious fanaticism against his 'le fanatisme du patriote', he contrasted civic virtue with ecclesiastical. 'On ne peut rien produire de grand sans ce zèle outré qui grossissant les objets, enfle aussi les espérances et met au jour des prodiges incroyables de valeur et de constance.'[1] In 1755 his 'enlightened' interpretation of Bacon was published, l'*Analyse de la philosophie du chancelier Bacon*. A year later he intelligently defended the ideas of Diderot and Rousseau in his polemical *Revue des feuilles de M. Fréron*, in which he continued their dialogue on virtue and society. So Deleyre rapidly became an active and convinced member of the group of encyclopaedists.

One can see what this meant for him when the dialogue between Rousseau and Diderot developed into a struggle and ended in a quarrel. How could he live when everything seemed to have collapsed around him? What was lacking was that point of contact between revolt and progress, between violence and persuasion, which the *Encyclopédie* had provided for him. 'Le sublime de l'amitié' transformed itself, under his eyes, into the sour violence of reciprocal accusations. Deleyre suffered another religious crisis. On 28th October 1758, he explained to Rousseau how their common revolt against the world which surrounded them now found its main *nourissement* in the disappointment they both felt in the group of *philosophes*, whom they judged unable to personify the ideal human society of free and equal men. 'Pourquoi déclamer encore contre les philosophes? Par la raison que j'ai déclamé quelquesfois contre les dévots et les théologiens, n'est ce pas? C'est que vous avés été trompé comme moi. Voilà ce qui me tue, cher citoyen. Si vous ne trouvés pas des âmes droites et justes, qui peut se flatter d'en rencontrer?'[2]

Exile was the only possible course. His pessimism became deeper

[1] *Encyclopédie*, vol. VI, p. 401.

[2] Jean-Jacques Rousseau, *Correspondance complète*, edited by R. A. Leigh, vol. V, Geneva, 1967, no. 720, p. 195.

and deeper. He wandered around Europe for ten years looking for a new path to follow. He succeeded in expressing his search by criticizing the situations with which he came into contact, whether it be Austria or Italy. He admired the models for revolt which were emerging, such as that of Pasquale Paoli about which he spoke with Boswell at Parma. He, too, took part in the crisis which seized all the French intellectuals in the last years of the reign of Louis XV. Moreover, he succeeded in expressing these feelings and thoughts in a more effective political form than many of his contemporaries.[1] As early as 1756, it had already seemed to him that Diderot had made too many concessions in his article on *Autorité politique*. 'La fin de cet article', he said, 'ne répond pas au commencement. Il ne faut pas toucher à ce qu'on ne peut pas manier à son gré.' He could no longer forgive Diderot for having written 'qu'on a contre les rois ambitieux, injustes et violens, que le parti de la soumission et de la prière'. 'Pour peu qu'une âme forte montre de foiblesse', he concluded, 'elle détruit son propre ouvrage.'[2] This enables us to measure how rapidly the process of political radicalization was taking place among some, at least, of the encyclopaedists. A homage to the absolutist tradition which seemed normal in 1751 aroused indignation in 1756. Two years later, in 1758, Deleyre, now in voluntary exile, published in the *Journal encyclopédique* some 'Pensées d'un républicain sur les mœurs de ce siècle'. This was a veritable manifesto which reflected the conclusions he had reached.[3] His social and moral protests were closely linked. 'Vous me montrez de palais, des statues, des arts analysés, des sciences perfectionnées, mais j'entens pousser des soupirs. Cent mille infortunés rejettent leur infortune sur cette vaine apparence de félicité: qu'est-ce donc notre philosophie?' He had seen the reverse of the medal. He found luxury more and more repugnant, not only as an injustice, but as an increasingly grave threat to liberty. In the end, the rich would crush the poor. 'L'esclavage civil mène bientôt au politique.' The revolt against tyrants, old and new, was more than legitimate. Classical recollections crowded his memory, from Porsenna to Brutus. It was

[1] On Pasquale Paoli, see *Boswell on the Grand Tour: Italy, Corsica and France. 1765–1766*, edited by F. Brady and F. A. Pottle, London, 1955, p. 48.

[2] Jean-Jacques Rousseau, *Correspondance complète*, vol. IV, 1967, no. 415, p. 21, letter dated 3 July 1756.

[3] October 1758, pp. 86 ff.

the kings who led their people to wars and disasters. Why shouldn't they answer personally for the consequences? 'Si jamais ma patrie étoit assiégée, je ne dis point que j'eusse absolument le courage d'imiter le brave Mucius, mais je trouverois bien grand qui l'oseroit faire.'

Deleyre was destined to strike the French monarch with his own hands, and without any hesitation or wavering. His was among the votes of the Convention which condemned Louis XVI to death.[1] 'Les rois sont des êtres insociables et hors de la nature...Écoutez-les eux-mêmes, ils tiennet leur autorité de Dieu...Puisque les rois se croient d'une autre espèce, ne les regardez pas comme de la vôtre...' These were his words on that day. The struggle between king and people was not in the least juridical or formal. For him it was, as Diderot and Rousseau had taught him, the clash between omnipotent nature and the mean inventions of men. 'Quoi! Celui qui mesure les mondes et pèse les astres, qui dompte les vents et franchit les mers, qui règne en quelque sorte sur tous les élémens s'abaisse jusqu'à ramper aux pieds d'un être souvent le plus vil de son espèce!' All his life is summed up in this speech and condemnation; even his experiences as a young provincial reappear: 'Paris, ville d'or et de sang, quand seras-tu de briques?'

From 1758 to 1793, from the *Pensées d'un républicain* to the guillotine, thirty-five years had passed. It would be worth our while to follow Deleyre step by step along his lonely road. We should see the accumulation of those thoughts which transformed a *philosophe* into a Jacobin. As we witness his aversion or his rebellion, his melancholy or his renunciation, every experience of his would lead us to a hidden corner of the world of the encyclopaedists. We should find ourselves in contact with those contrasts and contradictions which were developing between Rousseau and Diderot, between the France of the *Contrat social* and the Italy of Beccaria. They were to lead to the outbreak of the revolution. Deleyre, with his angry sensibility and his cosmopolitan culture, is one of the best witnesses of the transformation which few others experienced so intensely.

He was always deeply convinced that 'la liberté naîtra du sein de

[1] *Opinion d'Alexandre Deleyre, député du département de la Gironde sur la question du jugement de Louis XVI*. Paris (Convention nationale), n.d.

l'oppression'.[1] Tyranny would eventually strike and wound not only the ideas of the intellectuals, but would also harm something much deeper and widespread, namely, the most elementary feelings of the ordinary people. When that day came there would be no hope for tyranny. When virtue was involved, when absolutism was confronted by the resentment of those who considered themselves offended, when the rebellion of the ordinary man had begun, nothing could save despotism, 'car la vertu s'aigrit et s'indigne jusqu'à l'atrocité. Caton et Brutus étoient vertueux, ils n'eurent qu'à choisir qu'entre deux grands attentats, le suicide ou la mort de César.'[2]

Deleyre describes very well the psychological mechanism which led from Rousseau to the sansculottes,[3] especially since he was perfectly aware that the idea of virtue itself was changing at that time, under the influence of economic life. It was no longer a time for ancient republican moderation, but for a new morality, born of an overriding desire for new profits. 'La frugalité que les républicains observent par vertu, les manufacturiers doivent la garder par avarice.'[4] It was this very mixture of ancient and new morality, of traditional and modern customs which was producing ever deeper and more violent reactions in an increasing number of people.

When the revolution came, he was one of those who felt how much the new situation had in common with the ideas of the *philosophes*. 'La liberté vient de frapper aux portes des tombeaux...Montesquieu, Voltaire, Rousseau, Diderot, paroissent...Les voilà ces jours de la régéneration que vous avez prédite et préparée, lumières de la France et du monde...Voyez ces milliers d'hommes, armés tous à la fois, comme dans un seul jour, pour défendre cette liberté qu'ils ont conquise pour vous, sans même vous connoître...Soyez bénis de ce miracle unique dans l'histoire du monde.'[5] Republican virtue had taken root in absolutist France, whatever initial doubts there had been, and in spite of the fact that Rousseau had denied the possibility

[1] *Tableau de l'Europe pour servir de supplément à l'Histoire philosophique des établissements et du commerce des Européens dans les deux Indes*, Maestricht, 1774, p. 55.

[2] *Ibid.* p. 40.

[3] Cf. the fundamental work by Albert Soboul, *Les sansculottes parisiens en l'an II. Mouvement populaire et gouvernement révolutionnaire, 2 juin 1793–9 thermidor an II*, Paris, 1958.

[4] *Tableau de l'Europe*, p. 103.

[5] Alexandre Deleyre, *Essai sur la vie de M. Thomas*, Paris, 1791, pp. 289–90.

of its ever occurring. As the *Décade philosophique* observed when he died in 1797, Deleyre had been 'républicain par sentiment et par principes', giving an increasingly political and passionate form to the ideas he had absorbed from his encyclopaedist masters.[1]

The example of Deleyre has taken us a long way, even as far as the culmination in revolution of those sentiments and attitudes which had been fermenting in mid-century Paris. But evidently the relationship between the *philosophes* and the republican tradition can, and indeed must be, considered at a different level—not that of a virtue lost, wounded, and reconquered, but of constitutional forms, of the contact and contrast between the political ideas of the Enlightenment and the republican institutions still existing in the second half of the eighteenth century. So, we must return to Jean-Jacques Rousseau and his rapprochement between equality and the patrician Genevan republic. We must go back to the part he played in the political struggles between the *négatifs* and the *représentants* at the beginning of the sixties. It is a well-known story and has recently been very competently re-examined by Jean-Daniel Candaux in his presentation of the *Lettres écrites de la montagne*.[2] On the ideological front, Rousseau's paradox began to bear fruit. The ideas of contract, equality and democracy found their first concrete embodiment, their first political substance, in the republican tradition, in the Genevan reality, set in motion by the contrast between patrician and bourgeois. It is useful to read the *Contrat social* with Geneva in mind. Of course one would not do so to achieve an identification between Rousseau's political vision and the reality of the city of Calvin, but rather to see how a closer rapport between ideals and facts, between hopes and reality, was being established. Naturally, it is even more interesting to read the *Lettres écrites de la montagne* and observe how Jean-Jacques tried to interpret and solve the struggle within the Genevan republic.

To a large degree, this conflict followed the model we know well, the one common to all the republics in the period under discussion. It began in 1707. It was resumed in 1734, and again at the beginning of the sixties. The political monopoly of the patricians was disputed in an attempt to give power and strength to the mass of citizens, to those

[1] *Décade philosophique*, 10 germinal, an V (30 March 1797), p. 44.

[2] Jean-Jacques Rousseau, *Œuvres complètes*, pp. clix ff., 1575 ff.

who formed the bourgeoisie. The conflict continued, without any solution, culmination or outcome. Externally, it provoked the intervention of the great states on the borders. Internally, it brought to the fore the political claims of the people, of those who were neither patrician nor bourgeois, but *habitants*, *natifs* as they were called in Geneva. Both extremes, the nobility and the people, tended to unite against the bourgeoisie, but it was a precarious alliance, and did not help in re-establishing an equilibrium. In the end, everyone hoped for intervention from outside. Thus the conflicts deepened, in successive waves, within the little republic. The only limit was imposed by the international situation of which it was part. The history of Geneva in those years is exemplary. One could say it represents one of the most pure and perfect experiences of the republican phenomenon in the late eighteenth century. There are four reasons for this. First, foreign intervention in this long 'guerre civile de Genève', as Voltaire called it, remained particularly considerate and discreet. It was very different from the Prussian, French, or even the English in Holland, and even more so from the Russian, Austrian and Prussian in Poland, or the Napoleonic intervention in Venice, Genoa, Lucca or Ragusa. Secondly, the temptation to put an end to internal conflicts by becoming a monarchy was almost non-existent in Geneva. There was no wish to accept a dictator, a stadtholder, as in Holland, or a royal arbiter, as in Poland. Thirdly, the attention of all the most important thinkers of the age was rapidly being focused on the city of Calvin. One has only to recall, besides Rousseau, d'Alembert and Voltaire. These men succeeded in giving a universal significance to this little struggle. Geneva is also exemplary in a fourth and unhappier sense. The ancient republics in the second half of the eighteenth century could not be reformed. No one succeeded in finding a political mechanism capable of preventing the repetition of the conflicts between the nobility, bourgeoisie, and people. No way was found of formalizing these conflicts in institutions. They became chronic, and always threatened the very existence of the republic in the end. This is what happened in Geneva.

A compromise was reached in 1768. It seemed to favour the bourgeoisie; it made some concessions to the *natifs*, but it did not undermine the power of the patricians. The reaction came in 1782.

Intevention by the neighbouring monarchies became more intense and series of conflicts occurred which, as is known, ended by involving Geneva in the vortex of the French revolution. There was a prophecy and a hint of the destiny of the Low Countries and of the Italian republics. Each, in its own way, showed itself incapable of solving its internal problems. Then came the day when they found themselves confronted by a republic, the French one, very different in form and appearance, and were overwhelmed by it.

When that day came, at the end of the century, many of their citizens began to translate, read or re-read the works of Jean-Jacques Rousseau. They sought an explanation of the events which had involved and overcome them. Nor were they disappointed. Those pages contained an attempt to interpret the internal contrasts of Geneva, together with its entire constitutional history, in a new and more ample light. In his *Lettres* he stated he had taken 'Genève pour modèle des institutions politiques à fin de la proposer en exemple à l'Europe'.[1] In reality, he achieved the reverse. He gave a European significance to what was happening in his own city.

First of all, he saw it as a return to first principles. Geneva, too, should reform itself to conform to its real constitution. It should go back to the period of the origins of the republic, even before the epoch of the Protestant reformation. There Geneva would re-discover that just division of political power which had been lost in the sixteenth century under the rule of a few noble families. Rousseau rediscovered the roots of the republican idea itself in this return to first principles and established an effective point of contact between the re-emerging democratic ideas and the epoch of the medieval communes. Indeed, for a while, he did not seem able to free himself from this tradition, as was also the case within the republics, from Genoa to Amsterdam. The medieval past seemed to swallow up the more modern ideas of equality and liberty. Although he categorically denied any idea of the division and balance of power in his *Contrat social*, his final conclusion in the *Lettres* was that 'le meilleur gouvernement est celui dont toutes les parties se balancent dans un parfait équilibre'. Thus his authority served to support the very mechanism of the immobility of the ancient republics, the very factor which prevented them from freeing them-

[1] *Lettres écrites de la montagne* in *Œuvres complètes*, p. 809.

selves from the struggles of family, group, caste and class and engaging in a more modern, political struggle.[1]

But he yielded only for a moment. In reality, the idea of sovereignty, as Rousseau conceived it, gave a new and different base to the republican idea. Rousseau's contribution was very important, but only in the long run. It could not be decisive in the sixties. It gave a general significance to the conflicts, but did nothing to solve them. He himself realized this, and withdrew from the contest. He preserved only a personal consolation after this renewed spiritual contact with his own country. When he had to give up his citizenship in 1763, he said that 'ma patrie en me devenant étrangère ne peut me devenir indifférente'.[2] The image of a city in which virtue was rooted in a long tradition never left him. His example inspired an even greater number of his contemporaries.

Voltaire's part in these conflicts, so lucidly examined by Peter Gay, is remarkable, above all, for the agility and adaptability shown by the old philosopher.[3] He followed the spreading of the disputes. From the nobility, he passed to the bourgeois, and from them, to the people. He did not identify himself with any of them, but never lost touch completely. As always, he showed extraordinary intelligence, but not even he could find a way out, or an equilibrium. In the end he, also, was obliged to take refuge in general principles, in his *Idées républicaines*, and in his dialogue called *A.B.C.*[4] He made an effort to pass from Genevan politics to ideas of liberty, toleration, and even of equality, but he never completely succeeded. Some of the finest pages of Voltaire's political thought are to be found here; but the nature of the Genevan conflicts, the ancient, historical pretensions of the classes and castes of the republic still eluded every attempt to interpret and assimilate them. Geneva continued to be a stimulus, a pretext for Voltaire's thinking, but it did not fundamentally modify its course. His gaze remained fixed on Paris, on the struggles against

[1] *Ibid.* p. 844.

[2] Jean-Jacques Rousseau, *Correspondance générale*, vol. IX, p. 284, letter dated 12 May 1763.

[3] Nicola Matteucci, *Jacques Mallet-Du Pan*, Naples, 1957, and Peter Gay, *Voltaire's politics. The poet as realist*, Princeton, 1959.

[4] François-Marie Arouet de Voltaire, *A.B.C., dialogue curieux traduit de l'Anglais de monsieur Huet* (Geneva), 1762 (1768); *idem*, *Idées républicaines par un membre d'un corps* (Geneva, 1765).

the parliaments, on the crisis of the last years of the reign of Louis XV, on the attempt to organize public opinion around an increasingly compact group of *philosophes.* Voltaire knew that that was to be the decisive battlefield for the thinkers of the Enlightenment, within the great French monarchy, the very foundation of absolutism. Yet the weight of republican tradition and problems weighed heavily on him also. It compelled him to re-examine the basis of his political concepts. He did so particularly in the dialogue, *A.B.C.*, which is, fundamentally, a reflection on the problems we have been examining so far.[1] At first sight it is, above all, a eulogy of England, its freedom and its Whig tradition. This part is sustained and illustrated by the speaker, designated by the letter A. At the same time, he wants to attack the traditional conception of aristocracy, personified in this dialogue by speaker C. 'Pour moi, je n'aime que l'aristocratie...Je ne saurais souffrir que mon perruquier soit législateur. J'aimerais mieux ne porter jamais de perruque...Le gouvernement de Venise est le meilleur: cette aristocratie est le plus ancien état de l'Europe. Je mets après lui le gouvernement de l'Allemagne. Faites-moi noble vénitien on comte de l'Empire; je vous déclare que je ne peux vivre joyeusement que dans l'une ou dans l'autre de ces deux conditions.' The third speaker, B., is intent on escaping from this dilemma, either the English monarchy or the republics of the past. It is the Enlightenment which makes it possible to overcome this conflict. It gives man faith in his own epoch, makes him consider it better than antiquity and the past. It is the *philosophe* who gives a new meaning to the idea of human nature, who fights against superstition, who persuades men to accept a society in which even wigmakers, as, indeed, all those who work and produce, can be free and politically active. English freedom remains a model, but it is distant, and always in danger. It was certainly necessary to fight to preserve it. Now there was the danger from the civil war which was beginning to appear in the American colonies. ('Arrangez-vous avec vos colonies et que la mère et les filles ne se battent pas.')[2] But, above all, it was a question of invigorating this new sense of democracy which the modern world seemed to have brought to maturity. 'Allons au fait. Je vous avouerai que je

[1] *L'A.B.C., dialogue curieux traduit de l'Anglais de monsieur Huet. Sixième entretien. Des trois gouvernements et de mille erreurs anciennes* (Geneva), 1762.

[2] *Ibid. quinzième entretien. De la meilleure législation.*

n'accommoderais assez d'un gouvernement démocratique...J'aime à voir des hommes libres faire eux-mêmes les lois sous lesquelles ils vivent, comme ils ont fait leurs habitations...Aucun laboureur, aucun artisan, dans une démocratie n'a la vexation et le mépris à redouter...Être libre, n'avoir que des égaux c'est la vraie vie, la vie naturelle de l'homme.'[1]

These are the conclusions Voltaire draws from his Genevan experience. He had gone further than Rousseau. He had even gone so far as to defend the *natifs* against the bourgeoisie. But he had been able to do that because he was not so involved with the city as Rousseau, who, as long as he could, had defended his city and the republican tradition. Voltaire was a foreigner and acted like one. He had some connections with the course pursued by French diplomacy, and always assumed, whether independently or with support, the position of a foreign power obliged by circumstances to interfere in the affairs of the city. Therefore, his contribution was both more democratic and less republican. He found in Geneva a confirmation of the Enlightenment, whereas Rousseau had found an incitement to seek virtue.

The Genevan dispute was still continuing, when the two men found themselves at grips with yet another example of the varied mingling of the republican tradition and the renewed ideal of virtue. The case of Corsica was particularly curious. Many concerned themselves with it, among them Alexandre Deleyre. Rousseau's contribution is famous.[2] How could it have been possible for him and his contemporaries not to be concerned in this revolt against the Genoese aristocracy? It was an anti-colonial rebellion which had assumed the appearance of a conflict of the pure against the corrupt, of the poor against the rich, of the people of the land against the people of the city, of an oppressed nation against those who claimed the right to govern from afar. In some ways, it went beyond the stretch of sea separating the island from Genoa. It was the continuance of the struggle between nobility and people, which had brusquely re-emerged in 1746. After the insurrection at Genoa, an attempt at reconciliation was made, but, in the end, every innovation was suffocated. By the 1760s, only Pasquale Paoli and his followers carried on the

[1] *A.B.C., sixième entretien.*

[2] *Projet de constitution pour la Corse* in *Œuvres complètes*, tome III, pp. 899 ff., and comments by Sven Stelling-Michaud, *ibid.* pp. cxcix ff., 1726 ff.

fight.[1] French policy had favoured the aristocracy half way through the century. Now it tried to take advantage of the situation to impose its own power, in competition with England. It wished to annex the island, and, in fact, succeeded exactly two centuries ago, in 1769. In short, here was an extreme and impressive example of the ever-present internal conflicts of the ancient republics in eighteenth-century Europe. As such, it could hardly fail to arouse the men of the Enlightenment. Although Buttafoco wished Corsica to be a 'mixed republic', that is, aristocratic and protected by France, Rousseau's starting point was again a constitution without a hereditary nobility, without aristocratic castes. 'La loi fondamentale de votre institution doit être l'égalité.'[2] This did not mean there were to be no internal distinctions. 'Nous verrons comment on peut graduer chez un peuple différents ordres sans que la naissance et la noblesse y entrent pour rien.'[3] He intended to replace the traditional subdivisions with an egalitarian society which would also be able to generate differentiation between those who carried out distinct political tasks. The Corsican nation would be divided 'en trois classes, dont l'inégalité toujours personnelle pouvait être heureusement substituée à l'inégalité de race ou d'habitation qui résulte du système féodal municipal que nous abolissons'.[4] Candidates, patriots and citizens would be the three phases and the three degrees of political participation determined by age, property and social function, and not by hereditary rights of any kind. It would be a rural society, closed and self-sufficient, in which ancient ranks and orders would be dissolved.

One has only to look at Corsica a generation later to see the importance of this egalitarianism, a consequence of the struggle of the Corsican rebels against the Genoese nobility and rule. At the time of the French revolution, although the government attempted a reconciliation with Pasquale Paoli, the latter became more and more the dictator of the island, the indispensable arbiter in the struggles between factions, groups and families, while amongst the opposition

[1] Chauncey Brewster Tinker, *A new nation in Nature's simple plan. A phase of radical thought in mid-eighteenth century*. Princeton, 1922; George Pomeroy Anderson, 'Pascal Paoli, an inspiration to the sons of liberty' in *Massachusetts Historical Society. Proceedings*, vol. XXVI, and *Illuministi italiani*, VII, pp. 719 ff.

[2] *Projet de constitution pour la Corse*, p. 909.

[3] *Ibid.* p. 910.

[4] *Ibid.* p. 919.

an increasingly egalitarian commitment was increasing in strength in small but active groups of Jacobins. Filippo Buonarroti, the friend of Babeuf, was educated politically in Corsica which provided him with one of the first inspirations for his ideas on 'égalité de fait'.[1]

Following the evolution of similar ideas we could pass on from Geneva and Corsica to Poland, the American colonies, Holland and Switzerland and even to the relationships between the Italian republics and France in the epoch of the Directoire. But if we did so, we should have to reconsider the history of the last thirty years of the eighteenth century, and retrace the different phases of that 'age of democratic revolution', to use the title of R. R. Palmer's book.[2] These two large and fascinating volumes do just that most effectively. So I shall stop at the threshold of the new age, when the signs heralding the revolutions of the end of the century are still few and far between. Yet I don't think I am mistaken if I say that what we have examined so far, from the Puritan revolution of the seventeenth century onwards, may also be useful and important for understanding 'the age of democratic revolution'.

It may even alter the perspective from which R. R. Palmer studied it. 'Democratic' is certainly a sufficiently all-embracing word to include the Genevan disorders, the taking of the Bastille, the revolt of Belgium against Joseph II, the Polish revolutions and the formation of the United States of America. But, as this list shows, it is also too general a word. It includes far too many disparate phenomena. It is a general category of political thought. It is not an historically operative force with its roots in the past, opening on to a new reality and revealing all its internal contradictions. I am convinced that it is more worthwhile to follow the involvement, modifications and dispersion of the republican tradition in the last years of the eighteenth century, than to examine the emergence of the idea of democracy in those same years. Until the French revolution, this idea remained a concept rather than a force, a political form without effective political content.

From this point of view, Poland is particularly important. In recent

[1] Alessandro Galante Garrone, *Buonarroti e Babeuf*, Turin, 1948, pp. 52 ff.

[2] R. R. Palmer, *The age of democratic revolution: a political history of Europe and America, 1760–1800*, vol. I, *The challenge*, vol. II, *The struggle*, Princeton, 1959 and 1964.

years, admirable work has been done, both in Poland and elsewhere, which helps us to understand more clearly the attempts at reform, the revolts and the wars, the foreign intervention and the influence of the ideas of the Enlightenemnt there in the eighteenth century. From Jean Fabre to Bogusław Leśnodorski and Emanuel Rostworowski, to name only a few, we witness one of the most exciting and important pages of modern European historiography. They have brought to life for us once more problems and events which have been neglected for far too long as a result of the long-standing, rooted conviction that the period contained only the death-throes of a dying organism, the confused manifestations of an incurable anarchy.[1] In studying these historians, it immediately becomes clear that the prolonged tragedy of eighteenth-century Poland has much in common with the fate of the republics in Europe in the age of the Enlightenment. The constitution of the Sarmatic age was dominated by the profound conviction that it could not be modified or reformed. Poland was peaceful and static during the tempests of the northern wars, and increasingly lost control of its own policies. The golden liberty survived. 'Elementum meum libertas', as Stanislas Leszczyński said.[2] It was founded on the magnates who had the real power, and on the nobility which increasingly relied on its ability to impede any movement or transformation. The possible ways out of this immobility lead in the direction either of a constitution on the English model, or an 'enlightened liberty' which gained ground in Poland as she became influenced by the Europe of the Enlightenment, or else the acceptance of an enlightened despotism from outside, especially from the Russia of Catherine II. Stanislas Leszczyński, from his exile in Nancy, tries to indicate

[1] Jean Fabre, *Stanislas-Auguste Poniatowski et l'Europe des lumières*, Paris, 1952; Bogusław Leśnodorski, *Polscy jakobini*, Warsaw, 1960 (in French: *Les jacobins polonais*, Paris, 1965); Emanuel Rostworowski, 'Républicanisme sarmate et les lumières' in *Studies on Voltaire and the eighteenth century*, vols. XXIV–XXVII, 1963, pp. 1417 ff.; *idem*, 'La Suisse et la Pologne au XVIIIe siècle' in *Échanges entre la Pologne et la Suisse du XIVe au XIXe siècle*, Geneva, 1964; *idem*, 'Voltaire et la Pologne' in *Studies on Voltaire and the eighteenth century*, vol. LXII, 1968, pp. 101 ff.; *idem*, *The Commonwealth of the gentry*, in *History of Poland*, edited by A. Gieysztor, S. Kieniewicz, E. Rostworowski, J. Tazbir, H. Wereszycki, Warsaw, 1968, pp. 272 ff. Of notable interest are also: Ryszard W. Wołoszyński, *Polska w opiniach francuzów XVIII w.*, Warsaw, 1964, and *idem*, 'La Pologne vue par l'Europe au XVIIIe siècle' in *Acta Poloniae historica*, XI, 1965, pp. 22 ff.

[2] Frontispiece of his work *La voix libre du citoyen, ou observations sur le gouvernement de la Pologne*, n.p., 1749.

another, different way. This was to be an alliance of all the European republics against despotism, and hoped to enjoy the good-will and support of France.[1] Around 1763 he wrote: 'L'Europe n'est-elle pas partagée en deux sortes de gouvernement? Un est monarchique, comme la France, l'Espagne, Portugal, Naples, Sardaigne, Danemark, la Prusse, et la Russie, sans compter les petits états d'Italie et de l'Allemagne que composent le Corps germanique. Les gouvernements républicains sont: l'Angleterre, la Hollande, la Suède, la Pologne, Venise, les Cantons suisses et Gênes. En entrant dans les véritables intérêts de ces républiques, on conviendra que l'esprit de conquête ne les agite pas, qu'elles ne sont jalouses et attentives qu'à conserver ce qu'elles possèdent, à conserver la forme de gouvernement et surtout une pleine jouissance de leur liberté. Et surtout, comme ces États républicains n'ont jamais aucune prétention les uns sur les autres, serait-il difficile de les porter à une éternelle alliance pour le maintien de la paix et la conservation de leurs privilèges?...'[2]

But it was a utopia. The situation in Poland really resulted from conservatism, from Russian despotism, or from the internal transformation of the nobles. These frequently made use of the ideas of Rousseau, Mably, Beccaria and Filangieri to defend their privileges. But, in the end, they created a culture of their own—the moral and intellectual world of the 'Polish Jacobins'. They proposed the creation of a new magistracy which could co-ordinate and rule over all the others, and the abolition of the anarchy of *liberum veto*. It was a solution of the problems of Poland along the lines we have already seen developed in Venice, Genoa and the United Provinces. They soon came round to evolving, also under French influence, ideas of a typically 'constitutional' kind. But foreign pressure remained a dominant element. It outdid and finally crushed what nevertheless remained the most original, energetic, and intelligent attempt in eighteenth-century Europe to reform an ancient republic, to find a way out of the constitutional deadlock which had finally immobilized them all.

[1] Emanuel Rostworowski, 'Stanislas Leszczyński et l'idée de la paix générale', in *La Lorraine dans l'Europe des lumières. Actes du colloque organisé par la Faculté des lettres et des sciences humaines de l'Université de Nancy (24–27 octobre, 1966)*, Nancy, 1968, pp. 51 ff. (a particularly important essay for the idea of the republic in the eighteenth century).

[2] *Ibid.* p. 65.

The propaganda of Stanislas Leszczyński is extremely interesting. It caused his son-in-law, Louis XV, a certain anxiety on account of its republican nature, at the very time of the French crisis half way through the century. Or we might consider again the writings of the abbé Coyer, who succeeded in giving republican ideas new vigour and exalting Poland's past, but also in advocating reform, in opposition to French absolutism. Naturally, one should consider most carefully all the development and work of the thinkers of the Polish Enlightenment and of the Polish Jacobins, Ugo Kołłątay, for example, in whom traditional ideas and thoughts deriving from the most advanced movements of the western Enlightenment, find a precarious and fascinating balance. These are some of the considerations which help us understand the intellectual and moral value of Poland's desperate attempt to survive, and to give an example of internal transformation. It ended not only under the violent impact of the neighbouring powers, but also because of the insuperable conflicts its magnates and its nobility, its elective kings and its social structure, finally provoked. In spite of its heroic effort, Poland also failed to overcome the final crisis of the ancient European republics.

The Dutch attempt to overcome the conflicts facing those who wanted to resolve the contradictions between the power of the stadtholder and the privileges of the traditional patriciate, also ended in failure, and was of much smaller proportions. Until the very last, regents, bourgeois and people in the United Provinces also seemed to react, albeit in new forms, according to ancient models, from the middle of the seventeenth century. Foreign intervention, with France supporting the patriots and the German states taking the part of the stadtholder, was hardly a surprise. As is known, it was so violent that it overwhelmed any independent development of political forces. It is certainly difficult to understand a revolution which was crushed so rapidly. But one can perhaps interpret these events more effectively if one considers them not only as projected towards the future, as a herald of, and preparation for the French revolution (however fair this assessment might be) but also as turning back to the past, towards the historical roots of the archaic European republics in the absolutist period.[1]

[1] Alfred Cobban, *Ambassadors and secret agents. The diplomacy of the first earl of Malmesbury at the Hague*, London, 1954; R. R. Palmer, *The age of democratic revolution*, vol. I, pp. 320 ff.

Evidently, the only successful revolution before the taking of the Bastille was that of the English settlers in the American colonies. The constitution of the United States of America opened a new epoch in the history of the republics and brings to an end the group of problems I have tried to examine. Yet one has only to be familiar with current discussion of the events in Massachusetts and the other colonies to realize that, in origin, the problems were not so very remote or different from those we have so far examined. Conservative revolution? Defence of traditional privileges? Puritan spirit or the ideas of the Enlightenment? Here, too, the history of political ideas can contribute. One has only to study Bernard Bailyn's admirable book *The ideological origins of the American revolution* to feel that we are on the right track. The link with the commonwealthmen, especially with Trenchard and Gordon, is proven. The importance of the European Enlightenment is established. The movement itself tends, at least at the beginning, to take the form of a return to first principles. 'The leaders of the revolutionary movement were radicals, but they were eighteenth-century radicals, concerned like the eighteenth-century English radicals not with the need to recast the social order, nor with the problems of economic inequality and the injustices of stratified societies but with the need to purify a corrupt constitution and fight off the apparent growth of prerogative power.'[1] The story of the way in which, from this starting point, the constitution of the United States was formed, the way in which, in spite of obstacles sometimes similar to those faced by the Genevans, the Poles, the Dutch and the Swiss, the new continent found a new and different solution, evidently belongs to a completely different historical cycle. But the heritage of the past was blended with the riches of the present.

[1] Bailyn, *The American revolution*, p. 283.

IV

THE RIGHT TO PUNISH

IN THE AUTUMN of 1756 a gentleman in Abruzzo wrote to his friend in Rimini. This gentleman was Romualdo Sterlich. In spite of his German name, he was a typical representative of the culture of that part of the kingdom of Naples. His friend's name, Giovanni Bianchi, was, in contrast, so ordinary that he generally used the more distinguished Latin transliteration, Janus Plancus. He was one of the most cultured of the doctors and scientists in that part of the Papal state. Sterlich told him he had come by a copy of a short French book entitled *Code de la nature ou le véritable esprit des lois*, and that he had read it with great curiosity. 'It would desire the abolition of the ownership of goods, and that everything should return to the community.'[1] It was the book by Morelly which is so well known today. This was the first expression of eighteenth-century French communism, and, under Diderot's name, had far-reaching echoes throughout the century, until the time of Babeuf's conspiracy.[2] We should not be surprised to find that a gentleman of Chieti in Abruzzo owned it less than a year after its publication. We find the *Code de la nature* in Naples, in the same period or a little later, in the hands of Antonio Genovesi and of Francescantonio Grimaldi. In Puglia, Giuseppe Palmieri owned it, and it is among the books quoted and discussed by Giovanbattista Almici in his expurgated edition of Puffendorf's work on laws of nature and of peoples: an edition which Almici brought into line with Catholic orthodoxy, published in Venice in 1757 and 1759.[3] It would be easy to go on to prove that Morelly was also studied in the less important centres, and was discussed where one would least expect. As far as I know, Romualdo Sterlich is the first to mention him in Italy. He is also the first to confute him. 'Those who demand

[1] Biblioteca Gambalunga, Rimini, Fondo Gambetti, *Letters to Giovanni Bianchi*. Cf. F. Venturi, *Settecento riformatore*, p. 588.

[2] Cf. the edition of the *Code de la nature*, edited by Gilbert Chinard, Paris, 1950, the Russian translation, by V. P. Volgin, Moscow, 1956, and especially Richard N. Coe, *Morelly. Ein Rationalist auf dem Wege zum Sozialismus*, Berlin, 1961, with a full bibliography.

[3] Cf. *Illuministi italiani*, vol. v, pp. 25, 180, 516, 542, 1094.

the impossible don't really want anything. If one wishes to be useful to man, one should be content to set right those things one can.'[1] The dialogue about utopia and reform was born and flourished in every corner of Europe, for the whole of the second half of the century.

Social enthusiasm, as Shaftesbury called it, helped to bring new life to the utopia. It became popular during the early discussions of the group who were compiling the *Encyclopédie*. One has only to look at the articles on either side of Diderot's *Autorité politique*, in the first volume. The *Abiens*, a Scythian people, filled Diderot with admiration 'par je ne sais quelle élévation de caractère et je ne sais quel degré de justice et d'équité dont ils se piquoient'. So did the *Bacchionites* who 'après avoir banni d'entre eux les distinctions funestes du *tien* et du *mien*...il leur restoit peu de chose à faire pour n'avoir plus aucun sujet de querelles et se rendre aussi heureux qu'il est permis à l'homme de l'être', and also the *Bédouins*, who 'n'ayant ni médecins ni jurisconsultes', had not 'd'autres lois que celles de l'équité naturelle et guère autres maladies que la vieillesse'.[2] The seeds of utopia were many, as one can see, in the years in which the first two volumes of the great dictionary were being published, and in which Rousseau was meditating on his discourses on sciences and the arts, and on inequality. In 1755, the *Code de la nature* by Morelly was published. Its starting point was Montesquieu, and it ended with the more mature communism of the mid-century. This new impulse of the Enlightenment continued to be influential in the following years. In every group of *philosophes*, there was at least one who had a secret sympathy for a world in which the fatal distinction between mine and thine either never existed or had been abolished. The number of people who were in some way inspired by the idea of the community of goods increased: Robinet, Carra, Rétif de la Bretonne, and, in Italy, Rufino Massa or Francesco Longano.[3]

In the very souls of some of the greater philosophers, this vision of a world without mine and thine never disappeared. One has only

[1] F. Venturi, *Settecento riformatore*, p. 588.

[2] Cf. F. Venturi, *Le origini dell'Enciclopedia*.

[3] A. Lichtenberger, *Le socialisme au XVIIIe siècle. Étude sur les idées socialistes dans les écrivains français du XVIIIe siècle avant la Révolution*, Paris, 1895; H. Girsberger, *Der utopische Sozialismus des XVIII. Jahrhunderts in Frankreich und seine philosophischen und materiellen Grundlagen*, Leipzig, 1924; *Illuministi Italiani*, vol. VII.

to recall Diderot who wrote his *Supplément au voyage de Bougainville* as soon as the tension of his immense encyclopaedic work had slackened. In the past, the idea of communism appeared to be sporadic and isolated. Now, for the first time, it was the origin of a current of thought. It crystallized at this time in the most diverse circles of the European Enlightenment, and became one of the permanent forms of the desire to 'trouver une societé dans laquelle il soit presque impossible que l'homme soit dépravé ou méchant', as Morelly says, in which the idea of good and evil itself was abolished.[1] Beyond the 'horreur et la folie de notre état policé', by means of the 'révolte du cœur et de l'esprit', they could succeed in transferring 'notre paradis dans le seul endroit où nous pouvons le faire, je veux dire dans ce monde', as Dom Deschamps concluded. 'Il suffit d'établir l'égalité morale et la communauté des biens sur l'inégalité morale et la propriété pour effacer de l'humanité tous les vices moraux qui y règnent.'[2]

It would certainly be interesting to follow this crystallization of the communist ideal in the eighteenth century in detail. The traditional utopia expanded and altered under the stimulus of this typical Enlightenment determination to create paradise on this earth, to create a completely human society which was egalitarian and free. A system of communal life for everyone was to supersede the small groups of the elect, be they saints or monks. 'L'énigme métaphysique et morale', as Deschamps was still saying, was finally to be solved in practice, and not simply in theory. The history of the passage from utopia to ideal, from the individual dream to the communist political movement, is certainly full of interest. The whole age of the Enlightenment could not be understood without it. However marginal it may seem at times, it is really one of the most irreversible, unchanging and lasting results the eighteenth century transmitted to the nineteenth. It is one of those mental forms which, once they are fixed and shaped, will never yield without long and difficult trials and struggles, and without contact with a long and complex historical process. After the middle of the eighteenth century, the idea that the abolition of property might change the very basis of human society, might abolish

[1] Morelly, *Code de la nature*, p. 160.

[2] Dom Deschamps, *Le vrai système, ou le mot de l'énigme métaphysique et morale*, edited by Jean Thomas and Franco Venturi, Geneva, 1939 (reprinted 1963), pp. 135, 140, 166.

all traditional morality and every political form of the past, was never again to disappear.[1] Thus, it would be exciting to seek the origins of this idea in the pages of Morelly and Dom Deschamps. The studies by Richard N. Coe on the former, and, above all, by Bronisław Baczko on the latter have re-opened the discussion, and have tried to answer a question which, however simple it may seem, is really very complex: how was the idea of modern communism born?[2]

It seems certain that the thought of Dom Deschamps is very important, from this point of view. I can still remember my surprise when I read the manuscript of this Benedictine in the 1930s, and found on every page, at the very source as it were, that idea which had by then invaded the world, which was transforming it and being deeply modified itself through contact with reality.[3] Jean Wahl and Bronisław Baczko have now given us an interpretation of his philosophy and thought.[4] We have only to wait for what Baczko has promised us, a general examination of the problem of material and moral order, and its relations with utopia and evil in the thought of the Enlightenment.

But I promised a political history of various aspects of the Enlightenment, not merely an ideological one. I don't wish to deny the importance of understanding how, half way through the eighteenth century, the idea of communism was formulated more fully and more confidently and with a universality it had never had before. Indeed, I personally am always astonished at the amount of intellectual effort which nowadays is being devoted to the understanding of the mental

[1] The discussion which took place in Paris at the time of the Directoire is specially interesting for the end of the eighteenth century. Cf., for example, the article entitled, 'De la propriété, de quelques philosophes qui l'ont attaquée et des hommes qui accusent de ces attaques tous les philosophes et la philosophie' in *Journal d'économie publique, de morale et de politique*, XXI, 30 ventôse, year V (20 March 1797).

[2] R. N. Coe, *Morelly* and Bronisław Baczko, 'Wstęp' in Dom Léger-Marie Deschamps, *Prawdziwy system, czyli rozwiązanie zagadki metafisyki i moralności*, edited by B. Baczko, Warsaw, 1967, pp. 23 ff. (This introduction, translated into French, is published in *Cahiers Vilfredo Pareto*, fasc. 15, 1968, pp. 5–49, 'Le mot de l'énigme métaphysique ou Dom Deschamps'.)

[3] F. Venturi, 'Przedmowa do polsckiego wydania *Prawdziwego systema* dom Deschampsa' in Dom Léger-Marie Deschamps, *Prawdziwy system...*, pp. 2 ff. (The Italian text, 'La fortuna di Dom Deschamps', in *Cahiers Vilfredo Pareto*, fasc. 11, 1967, pp. 47 ff.)

[4] Jean Wahl, 'Cours sur l'athéisme éclairé de Dom Deschamps' in *Studies on Voltaire and the eighteenth century*, fasc. LII, pp. 11 ff.

structures of the most remote peoples, to the understanding of the evolution of the most primitive mentalities, and even to the reconstruction of the most hidden mechanisms which accompany the very formation of civilization, incest and kinship, '*le cru et le cuit, le miel et les cendres*', in the words of Lévi-Strauss; while much less energy is devoted to understanding the origin of the ideas which concern us much more, such as communism, for example. This is the romantic return to the philosophy of the primitive, of *Ur*, which often prevents us from seeing the 'structures mentales' closer to us. It is easy to see why the best studies of the subject, such as the one by Bronisław Baczko, originate in Poland, or why the best studies of socialist ideas on the eve of the French revolution or of Fourier and Babeuf, such as those by L. S. Gordon, I. I. Zil'berfarb, V. M. Dalin or A. R. Ioannisjan, come to us from Russia. The problem of the birth and transformation of the utopia in the eighteenth century cannot help being alive in both these countries, even though the discussion of it seems to have died down recently.[1]

But this is not my concern here. It is rather the history of political ideas, the relationship between the forces of social enthusiasm, to quote Shaftesbury, the forces of the burgeoning utopias of a human society able to solve 'le mot de l'énigme métaphysique et morale' and the concrete determination to modify this or that aspect of the societies inherited from the past, to bring about practical change. In short, the relationship between utopia and reform.

Let us consider a problem which touches both poles of Enlightenment thought—the problem of the right to punish. Obviously this is related to the question of the individual and society, while, at the same time, it is also closely connected with the more specific history of methods, examples, instruments and practice, and of small changes. Thus, it involves, on the one hand, a discussion of principle and on the other, a consideration of concrete problems. It is this dual aspect of the problem which makes it particularly important for understanding

[1] See, for example, the collection of articles published by the Akademija nauk SSSR under the title: *Iz istorii social'no-političeskich idej. Sbornik statej k semidecjatipjatiletiju Ak., V. P. Volgina*, Moscow, 1955, and *Istorija socialističeskich učenij*, Moscow, 1962, where I. I. Zil'berfarb discusses some recent work on Fourier and where there are numerous studies of the utopists in the eighteenth and nineteenth centuries. Among the principal works: V. M. Dalin, *Grakch Babef nakanunie i vo vremja Velikoi francuzskoj revoljucii (1785–1794)*, Moscow, 1963.

the Enlightenment. One example will, perhaps, be enough to show its principal elements. We shall follow the reception of Beccaria's work *Dei delitti e delle pene* throughout Europe.[1] Everywhere it drew attention to the problem of the existence of crime itself and with the ways to repress it.

A small group of young men was forming in Milan at the beginning of the 1760s; it was known, half-jokingly, as the *Accademia dei Pugni*. Soon the internal tensions common to every Enlightened movement grew. Ten years before in Paris, the most notable example had been the discordant friendship of Jean-Jacques Rousseau and Diderot. Now, in Milan, their reading of the *Contrat social*, their continual polemic with their family, social and political surroundings also animated their internal arguments. From these were born some of the most important works of the Italian Enlightenment: the *Meditazioni sulla felicità* and the *Considerazioni sul commercio di Milano* by Pietro Verri, *Dei delitti e delle pene* by Cesare Beccaria, together with work published collectively by them and other members of this group, *Il Caffè*, a periodical which lasted two years. Beccaria and Verri may have exchanged positions, as happens in every authentic dialogue, but Beccaria ended by representing Rousseau, and Verri, Voltaire. At Milan also, however toned down by the favourable and temperate atmosphere, utopias and reforms polarized the attention of the spirits and minds of men in the 1760s.[2]

For thousands of years sin and crime, guilt and offence to society had been tied together in an intricate knot. It was now cut in one blow by Beccaria. If the church wanted, it could concern itself with sin. The state's task was only to estimate and make good the damage which the breaking of the law had caused the individual and society. The degree of utility or non-utility was the yardstick for all human actions. Punishment was not expiation. Judges should only restore the disturbed harmony. Penal law was to lose all its sacred content. Beccaria's radical thinking, implicitly but nonetheless definitively, denied every religious conception of evil, every original sin, all public sanctions of morality. His utilitarianism derived from a desire to create a society based on reason and calculation, and to destroy every

[1] Harlem (Leghorn), 1764.

[2] F. Venturi, *Settecento riformatore*, pp. 645 ff.

prejudice or obstacle inherited from the past. Bentham always acknowledged that Beccaria's book had been for him the most stimulating formulation of a thought which he was to take up and develop.

But how could there exist in such a society the right to punish and even to condemn to death? Beccaria, with an appeal which might well have been Rousseau's, made a criminal give the reasons for the rebellion, the revolt against all laws and oppressions. 'What are these laws I must respect, that they leave such a huge gap between me and the rich? Who made these laws? Rich and powerful men...Let us break these fatal connections...let us attack injustice at its source.'[1] Underlying Beccaria's reasoning was his doubt concerning 'the perhaps unnecessary right of property', as he put it, his vision of a society in which equality no longer existed only in juridical abstractions but was an economic reality.[2] On a personal level, Beccaria's aversion to the right to punish was profound. Not only did he feel horror at the thought of violence or cruelty, but his innermost being rejected all attempts to create a theory, or a justification for them. He constantly rejected any use made of them by states, societies or the law. His pages on the death penalty and on torture derive from this double difficulty, social and personal, in accepting the right to punish itself, and the consequences it inevitably involved. He affirmed that legislators and jurists 'should rule the lives and fortunes of men tremblingly'.[3] He was sincerely convinced that all his decisions would have a bearing on the fate of his fellows.

Beccaria was on the very threshold of the eighteenth-century utopia. He felt all its fascination: he felt drawn, by his logic and by his sentiments, towards a solution which would enable man to solve the problem of good and evil at its source, as he said. Yet Beccaria stopped on the threshold. He wanted reason and calculation to dominate the egalitarian and libertarian impulses in him, however strong they might be. One could wonder with what authority society claimed the right to punish, but this should not lead to the dissolution of society itself, or to the negation of law. He combined the ideas of Helvétius and Jean-Jacques Rousseau. His answer to the problem he had put himself was not a utopia, but a society of free and equal men.

[1] Beccaria, *Dei delitti e delle pene*, para. xxviii, 'Della pena di morte'.
[2] *Ibid.* para. xii (xxx in A. Morellet's reordering), 'Furti'.
[3] *Ibid.* 'A chi legge'.

Only a strictly utilitarian concept of society would make possible, in a practical sense, the achievement of equality. If a crime necessitated the making good of damage, everyone had the right and the duty to perform this task. All privileges of caste and group were only obstacles in the path of justice. In a similar way, as far as the wealth of society was concerned, utilitarian calculation was the only way to reach equality. He used a formula he probably got from the Scottish philosophers. Pietro Verri also used it at this time. All society should strive towards 'the greatest happiness divided by the greatest number'.[1] It was a rational formula for a programme of reform as opposed to utopian revolt.

Beccaria's book appeared in Leghorn in the summer of 1764. It did not bear its author's name. His friends in Milan who helped him publish it, waited in trepidation. Beccaria himself was worried. Then, for a moment, it seemed that the influence of Rousseau in this little book was so strong as to preclude its slow and gradual penetration. Even in Paris, the best journal of the age, the *Gazette littéraire de l'Europe*, said that *Dei delitti e delle pene* was nothing 'qu'un recueil des principales maximes du Contrat social...'[2] In Italy, the work was not received with astonishment, but with a violent denunciation. It was attacked by a strange friar, Ferdinando Facchinei, in an essay which appeared in Venice.[3] Facchinei had read Beccaria's work and was convinced that the very idea of a society of free and equal men was not simply a utopia, but a dangerous utopia. It was not simply a mistake, but an offence to allow oneself to be attracted by such a dream. How could one believe that a punch given to a general could be punished in the same way as one given to a porter? How could men be allowed to judge, according to a criterion of pure and simple utility, crimes which disrupted order itself, the moral and religious basis of all human society? In his work, Facchinei expressed not only his fear of the age-old rhythm of life changing, but, above all, of finding oneself

[1] Beccaria, *Dei delitti e delle pene*, 'A chi legge'.

[2] *Gazette littéraire de l'Europe*, 13 February 1765, pp. 301 ff., contained in Cesare Beccaria, *Dei delitti e delle pene. Con una raccolta di lettere e di documenti relativi alla nascita dell'opera e alla sua fortuna nell'Europa del Settecento*, edited by F. Venturi, Turin, 1965, p. 311.

[3] *Note e osservazioni sul libro intitolato Dei delitti e delle pene*, n.p. (Venice), 1765. Cf. Gianfranco Torcellan, 'Cesare Beccaria a Venezia', in *Rivista storica italiana*, 1964, III, pp. 720 ff.

alone, without the protection of religion, and confronted by increasingly horrible and cruel social realities. The ancient consolations which church and tradition had continued to administer through the centuries would vanish. As one reads the heavy and tiring pages of Father Facchinei against Beccaria, one can understand how deeply the reforms proposed by *Dei delitti e delle pene* penetrated the psychology and politics of that age. He foresaw upheaval and ruin if the ancient pillars of society were removed; torture, the inquisition, the death penalty, the unquestioned authority of ancient laws, the unquestioning respect for judges and courts. 'This book of such small size, is nevertheless full of long invective against legislators and princes, both ecclesiastical and lay, and especially against the sacred tribunal of the inquisition. It contains all the most enormous errors which blasphemy has ever produced against sovereignty and the Christian religion through the mouths of all the most impious heretics and all the irreligious men of both ancient and modern times.'[1]

Ferdinando Facchinei could only find two terms by which to describe his accusation of Beccaria, who had passed from religious to social criticism, whose arguments against the inquisition had led him to question the whole basis of the right to punish itself. Beccaria, for him, was: '*il Rousseau degli italiani*' and a '*socialista*'. The first, after what we have considered so far, is hardly surprising. The second continues to astonish readers who have been obliged to admit that this was probably the first time a modern language made use of the term 'socialist'. Hans Müller has recently re-examined the problem in a book of great fascination for anyone interested in the history of words and ideas.[2] He tells us that the word 'socialist', at first in Latin and then, rapidly, in Italian, was first used about the middle of the century. It seems to have been used for the first time by the German Benedictine, Anselm Desing, to indicate the current of natural law deriving from Puffendorf and Cumberland which placed the *socialitas*, the social instinct of man, at the very base of all natural law. According to the Catholic polemicist, these thinkers, these 'socialists' ended up by removing all religious elements from their

[1] Quoted from Beccaria, *Dei delitti e delle pene*, pp. 174–5.

[2] Hans Müller, *Ursprung und Geschichte des Wortes 'Sozialismus' und seiner Verwandten*, Hanover, 1967. For the word in Italian, see F. Venturi, 'Socialista e socialismo nell'Italia del Settecento' in *Rivista storica italiana*, 1963, I, pp. 129 ff.

vision of society, and by considering every human action solely from the point of view of society, ignoring revelation, religion and the church. He believed that this led the 'socialists' to resemble the 'naturalists', or even the Hobbesians; although the latter denied the existence of the *socialitas*, they also considered only earthly well-being, the 'commoda huius vitae'.[1] In his criticism of the concept of 'socialitas',[2] Desing states that the 'naturales socialistae', that is, Puffendorf and Cumberland, themselves admit that the Christian religion 'docet socialitatem veram'. Why then do they not put it at the centre of their doctrines?[3] In reality: 'Socialitas Puffendorffii caret capite, id est Deo'.[4] The same can be said for all the 'naturalistae';[5] they and the 'socialistae' attempt in vain to distinguish between natural law and revelation. 'Socialistae etiam religionem veram ac revelatam subjiciunt ac subordinant fini societatis',[6] concluding that 'sententia socialium non est apta ad refraenandos homines ab injustitia'.[7] On the contrary, 'doctrina socialium potius ad evertendam societatem nata est'.[8] They have in common with Hobbes the idea that natural law must only serve 'nudae conservationis commoda, quaedam in hac vita'.[9] Desing, in fact, knew nothing of Shaftesbury and his enthusiasm for the social cause but his word 'socialist' indicated that very current of thought, which, transformed into a lay and moralistic concept, found its expression in the English philosopher and deist. That same word, having passed from Latin to Italian, was first used in 1765 with regard to Beccaria. It no longer referred simply to someone who considered sociability as a constituent and primordial element in man. Inevitably it came to mean a writer who wanted a society of free and equal men, and who had been inspired by Rousseau. 'Everything our writer proposes...is based

[1] *Juris naturae larva detracta compluribus libris sub titulo juris naturae prodeuntibus, ut puffendorffianis, heineccianis, wolffianis etc.* Munich, 1753, 3 vols; Ildefons Stegmann, *Anselm Desing Abt von Ensdorf, 1699–1772. Ein Beitrag zur Geschichte der Aufklärung in Bayern*, Munich, 1929.

[2] Desing, *Juris naturae*, vol. I, p. 25.

[3] *Ibid.* p. 69. [4] *Ibid.* p. 75. [5] *Ibid.* p. 77.

[6] *Ibid.* p. 87. [7] *Ibid.* p. 97. [8] *Ibid.* p. 100.

[9] *Ibid.* p. 101. On the whole problem of 'socialitas' see J. N. Hert (Hertius), *De socialitate primo naturalis juris principio dissertatio* in *J. N. Hertii Commentationum atque opusculorum de selectis et rarioribus ex jurisprudentia universali, publica, feudali et romana nec non historia germanica argumentis tomi tres*', Frankfurt-am-Main, 1700, vol. I, pp. 88 ff.

entirely on the two false and absurd principles, that men are born free, and are all naturally equal'.[1] Poor and rich, docile and rebellious, strong and weak, men were anything but free and equal, and it was for this very reason that they needed an authority to guide and punish them. In its turn, this authority needed the support of torture and the death penalty to be effective, just as it needed, as its only possible justification, a supreme religious sanction. Without authority, compulsion, subordination and religion any human society was unthinkable. One had only to compare the state of nature to be convinced. Even in the state of 'primitive and natural liberty' it had been right to kill to defend one's own life. Facchinei affirmed that 'all the socialists agreed with this' as well. How could one imagine that, with the creation of laws, this primary right would lapse? It was certainly not possible, 'given the present state and condition of human nature, to form a society in which no one could be found so iniquitous as to be able to kill any one of his fellows for any reason at all. I don't believe a socialist would want to be so little well-disposed as not to agree that that was not possible.'[2] Social instinct would never prevail to such an extent that the necessity to repress crime would be relieved. Even the socialists would be obliged to accept such an interpretation. The utopia was impossible.

But why was there the death penalty? Beccaria, too, had refused to allow the social instinct, the 'socialitas', to lead to utopia. But, when confronted by the gallows, he had indicated a different solution to the problem. In the drawing he sketched out and sent to his publisher to be engraved for the third edition of his work, in 1765, there is a figure of Justice with the features of a Minerva, thus uniting law and wisdom. The figure recoils in horror from the severed heads the executioner is offering her, while she turns her benevolent and smiling gaze towards the instruments of work—shovels, saws, etc.[3] The death penalty was to be replaced by hard labour. Only in this way would society avoid commiting a juridical crime, and the criminal be

[1] Facchinei, *Note* quoted from Beccaria, *Dei delitti e delle pene*, p. 175.

[2] *Ibid.* p. 168.

[3] F. Venturi, 'L'immagine della Giustizia' in *Rivista storica italiana*, 1964, III, pp. 705 ff., with the additions and corrections of Luigi Firpo, 'Contributo alla bibliografia del Beccaria' (Le edizioni italiane settecentesche del *Dei delitti e delle pene*) in *Atti del convegno internazionale su Cesare Beccaria promosso dall'Accademia delle scienze di Torino* (4–6 October 1964), Turin, 1966, pp. 329 ff.

able to pay his debt to society. These would be the only socially useful ways of making amends.

The social implications of such a solution were gradually revealed during the debate on Beccaria's work which spread almost everywhere throughout Europe. To ask oneself whether hard labour was an adequate punishment for crime, was not only to wonder whether it could sufficiently frighten potential delinquents, or whether it was a practical solution, that is whether it corresponded to the fundamental exigencies of any repression of criminality. The most significant answers to *Dei delitti e delle pene* were not made on a technical penalistic plane. It was soon realized that Beccaria had really wished to respond not only to the need to humanize and improve the law, but that his thought was directed at the very centre of human society. It was easy to trace the reforms he proposed back to the potential utopia from which he had started. Father Facchinei had already realized that hard labour would be meaningful only if it was very different from free labour, and if the condition of the convict was substantially changed in relation to the man who had to work to earn his living. Yet, one had only to look around to realize, he said, that this difference did not exist. The poverty of those who worked was such that their situation was not very different from that which Beccaria proposed should be assigned to those sentenced to hard labour. 'From the life led by the imaginary murderer...to that of slaves there isn't even a single step...We have, before our eyes, the example of a great many people who freely lead a life harder than the hardest slavery.'[1] Every distinction between the life of those doing hard labour and the lives of the poverty-stricken tended to disappear. It was society itself, not the judge, which condemned the poor to the conditions in which they live.

The discussion took on a very different dimension when, in 1766, Beccaria's book was published in its French version by Morellet, and its author went to Paris to receive the praise of the *philosophes*. I do not propose to consider here the technical discussion the work provoked in France, which was indeed lively and varied. Fundamentally this was not the concern of men such as Morellet, Diderot, Voltaire or d'Holbach. What matters is their reaction to the dilemma, utopia or

[1] Facchinei, *Note*, pp. 172–3.

reform, which they all, in various ways, felt was implicit in Beccaria's book. Like many others, d'Alembert was impressed by the way the book wove together logic and precision 'et, en même temps, de sentiments et d'humanité',[1] reason and feeling, extremes which struck all the readers and which were the most visible aspect of Beccaria's attitude towards society, of his 'socialism' and utilitarianism. Melchior Grimm was not deaf to the appeal which the Milanese writer seemed to make more and more intense and urgent as he went on. Grimm said that, after this work, it was essential 'de remédier à la barbarie froide et juridique de nos tribunaux'.[2] Morellet strove to transform *Dei delitti e delle pene*, while translating, into a veritable *Traité*, a judicial system capable of being the basis of a new penal code. Beccaria had certainly had the ability, with his 'amour de l'humanité' and his 'sensibilité tendre', to bring about 'l'émotion dans l'âme de ses lecteurs'. 'Malheur aux hommes froids qui pourroient parler sans enthousiasme des intérêts de l'humanité: pourvu que cet enthousiasme ne nuise point à la solidité des raisons et qu'en se livrant aux mouvemens d'une éloquence séduisante on ne s'écarte pas du chemin de la vérité.'[3] Morellet affirmed that Beccaria had made precisely that mistake. His book should be re-structured according to a more logical, more classical and more systematic arrangement. He did this, and was accused by Diderot of having killed the book, of having destroyed its very spirit. 'Le protocole de la méthode dans un morceau où les idées philosophiques, colorées, bouillantes, tumultueuses, exagérées, conduisent à chaque instant l'auteur à l'enthousiasme.' Why not respect, in translating, those 'dissonances morales' which made the author pass 'de la fureur au calme', only to return, then, from reason to enthusiasm?[4] The discussion of the style of the work was widespread on both sides of the Alps at that time. Nor is there any doubt

[1] *Ibid.* p. 312. Letter from d'Alembert to Frisi, dated 9 July 1765.

[2] Beccaria, *Dei delitti e delle pene*, p. 320, taken from an article in the *Correspondance littéraire*, to be found, dated 1 August, 1765, in vol. VI of Maurice Tourneaux's edition, 1878, pp. 329 ff.

[3] Beccaria, *Dei delitti e delle pene*, p. 330. Morellet's version, under the title, *Traité des délits et des peines, traduit de l'Italien d'après la troisième édition, revue, corrigée et augmentée par l'auteur, avec des additions de l'auteur qui n'ont pas encore paru en Italien*, was published in 1766, Lausanne (Paris).

[4] Beccaria, *Dei delitti e delle pene*, p. 405, taken from the *Oeuvres complètes* of Diderot, edited by J. Assézat, vol. IV, Paris, 1875, pp. 60 ff.

that this examination also served to reveal the depths of Beccaria's thought and personality. Rousseau and Helvétius, feeling and calculation, were transparently present to all contemporaries, in the very way he expressed his thoughts.[1]

Voltaire was too deeply engaged in his battle against the injustices and cruelties of the parliaments to trace the origins of the book he admired so much. Even if he had been able to do so, he might not have been pleased with its sources. The temptation, the tension of a utopia were not for him. He took up Beccaria for what he said against the disorder and horror of the ruling legislation. He gave the task of examining and developing the more technical part to a lawyer he knew, Christin de St Claude, of Besançon. It was adapted to the French situation. Numerous pages of vigorous polemics were added, and then Voltaire published it all in 1766, in a great hurry, under the title of *Commentaire*. It was destined to become world-famous (it was, by the way, the first of Voltaire's works to be published in the American colonies).[2] It is useful to re-read, after having finished *Dei delitti e delle pene*, in one of the many editions which linked those works in a common destiny. By doing so, what the men of the Enlightenment had in common and the ways in which they differed in the mid-sixties becomes clear. Voltaire's paragraph on the death penalty is particularly characteristic. He does not commit himself totally to its abolition. For him it is a question of humanity and convenience, rather than a principle. 'Il est évident que vingt voleurs vigoureux, condamnés à travailler aux ouvrages publics toute leur vie, servent l'état par leur supplice et que leur mort ne fait de bien qu'au bourreau que l'on paye pour tuer les hommes en public.' The social implications of the problem are avoided, and their place taken by a generalized trust in the value of work. 'Forcez les hommes au travail, vous les rendez honnêtes gens.'[3] In Voltaire, the struggle against evil and injustice is

[1] *Ibid.* pp. 205 ff.

[2] Marcello Maestro, *Voltaire and Beccaria as reformers of criminal law*, New York, 1942; Ira O. Wade, 'The search for a new Voltaire. Studies in Voltaire based upon material deposited at the American Philosophical Society' in *Transactions of the American Philosophical Society*, new series, vol. XLVIII, 4 July 1958, pp. 86 ff.; Paul M. Spurlin, 'Beccaria's essay On crimes and punishments in eighteenth-century America' in *Studies on Voltaire and the eighteenth century*, vol. XXVII, 1963, pp. 1489 ff.

[3] Beccaria, *Dei delitti e delle pene*, p. 374, taken from the *Commentaire sur le traité. 'Des délits et des peines'*, para. x, *De la peine de mort.*

always to the point, entirely concentrated on this or that concrete aspect. It does not lead to general statements of principle. This can also be seen in his correspondence with Beccaria. Voltaire always tends to draw him into his battles, to make him his ally against the judges who condemned Calas or La Barre. 'De quelque côté qu'on jette les yeux, on trouve la contrariété, la dureté, l'incertitude, l'arbitraire.' He found his way through this legislative chaos better than anyone else, and knew how to fight with sharp, precise and suitable weapons. Whenever he reflected on the general significance of his battle, for example in the closing lines of his *Commentaire*, he saw the improvement of the jurisprudence as his goal, rather than the transformation of society itself by means of a new code of laws. 'Nous cherchons dans ce siècle à tout perfectionner, cherchons donc à perfectionner les lois dont nos vies et nos fortunes dépendent.'[1] When he looked beyond his daily struggles, the object of his polemics became religion. 'Quelle abominable jurisprudence que celle de ne soutenir la religion que par des bourreaux', he wrote to Beccaria on 30 May 1768. 'Voilà donc ce qu'on appelle une religion de douceur et de charité!'[2]

It is more difficult to understand the position of Diderot. The evidence on which an interpretation of his thought on this matter must be based is uncertain. Some, at least, of the marginal comments on Beccaria's work traditionally attributed to him are of dubious authenticity.[3] Diderot animatedly discussed these problems at the house of Baron d'Holbach, as we learn from the *Correspondance littéraire* of his friend, Grimm and with the Scottish painter, Allan Ramsay. When Ramsay sent him a letter refuting the fundamental claims of Beccaria's book, Diderot hastened to translate and circulate it. The refutation by the Scottish artist was radical. One should not enquire into the nature of human society to establish a just penal law. The concrete political traditions of every country should determine the nature of one's action, and also provide the weapons for the struggle against criminals. His vision was intended to be realistic, one might say Machiavellian. It was based on the assumption that force, necessity and chance are the basis of every government. It seemed to him that

[1] Voltaire, *Commentaire*, para. xxiii, in Beccaria, *Dei delitti e delle pene*, p. 379.

[2] *Ibid.* p. 451, taken from Voltaire, *Correspondence*, edited by T. Besterman, vol. LXIX, pp. 159 ff., no. 14090.

[3] Beccaria, *Dei delitti e delle pene*, pp. 397 ff.

the character of Beccaria's work was typically utopian: 'tout ouvrage spéculatif, tel que celui "Dei delitti e delle pene", rentre dans la catégorie des *utopies*, des *républiques de Platon* et autres politiques idéales, qui montrent bien l'esprit, l'humanité et la bonté d'âme des auteurs, mais qui n'ont jamais et n'auront jamais aucune influence actuelle et présente sur les affaires'.[1] His distrust of the reforming capacities of philosophy was also radical. It was useless to voice one's indignation, even more so to criticize. Circumstance and destiny determined the changes in the human condition. 'Les cris des sages et des philosophes sont les cris de l'innocent sur la roue, où ils ne l'ont jamais empêché et jamais ne l'empêcheront d'expirer, les yeux tournés vers le ciel...Ce n'est jamais la harangue du sage qui désarme le fort; c'est une autre chose, que la combinaison des événements fortuits amène.'[2] It was completely useless to protest or to reason. Utopia and reform both collapsed under this desperate scepticism, this implacable coldness. It is difficult to say to what extent Diderot, who often revealed great interest in Hobbes's thought, might have been influenced by this letter from Allan Ramsay. At the most, we can admit that the latter's crude realism helped to take him a step nearer to attempting to free himself from that sense of guilt which torture, the death penalty and the cruelty of society had inspired in Beccaria. It moved him in some way nearer to a more detached and dispassionate judgment on the origins and the nature of the right to punish, and on the implications of a good or bad penal law. Society was dominated by the determination of those who ruled to keep their power. Punishments were never inflicted in proportion to the harm caused by the crime, 'mais en raison de la sécurité des maîtres'.[3] In this perpetual struggle, how many of the evils were caused by the judiciary apparatus, and how many were caused by chaos, indifference and mere disorganization? 'Il y a environ dix-huit millions d'hommes en France, on ne punit pas de peine capitale trois cents hommes par an dans tout le royaume; c'est-à-dire que la justice criminelle ne dispose par an que de la vie d'un seul

[1] *Ibid.* pp. 543 ff., taken from D. Diderot, *Correspondance*, edited by Georges Roth, vol. v, Paris, 1959, pp. 244 ff. See a not very different version in D. Diderot, *Œuvres complètes*, vol. iv, pp. 52 ff. Cf. Alastair Smart, *The life and art of Allan Ramsay*, London, 1952.

[2] Beccaria, *Dei delitti e delle pene*, p. 545.

[3] *Ibid.* p. 406, taken from the *Œuvres complètes* of Diderot, edited by J. Assézat, vol. iv, Paris, 1875, pp. 60 ff.

homme sur soixante mille; c'est-à-dire qu'elle est moins funeste qu'une tuile, un grand vent, les voitures, une catin malsaine, la plus frivole des passions, un rhume, un mauvais, même un bon médecin . . . '[1] Diderot repeated similar thoughts to Catherine also, a few years later, in his *Observations sur le Nakaz*: 'Je ne prétends point à ôter au *Traité des délits et des peines* le caractère d'humanité qui lui a mérité un si grand succès. Je fais autant de cas que personne de la vie des innocents et mes opinions particulières ne peuvent que m'inspirer la plus grande commisération pour les coupables. Cependant je ne puis m'empêcher de calculer.'[2] Diderot evidently had no intention of defending in any way the cruelty of traditional justice, as he himself affirms. Instead, he intended to draw attention to the 'multitude d'inconvénients qui sont bien autrement graves et auquels on ne donne aucune attention'.[3]

We could say that Beccaria's social conscience tended to focus on the prisons and the gallows, while Diderot's tended to cover all aspects of human society. Since he had resolved on a greater detachment, his 'socialism' tended to become 'sociology'. These terms are perhaps too modern for this context. But one was already in use, as we have seen, and the activity which was soon to be called sociology was beginning in those very years of the eighteenth century, in Scotland and on the continent.

But didn't Diderot run the risk of reducing and deadening any reforming spirit in this way? He himself had doubts. He reconsidered his thoughts critically, but then found his justification at last in the affirmation that a truth should always be declared openly. But even this didn't seem to solve the question. In fact, in spite of Voltaire, in spite of Beccaria's influence and in spite of the good will of the philosophers in France, the reform to penal law proceeded slowly and uncertainly in the quarter of a century which followed the publication of *Dei delitti e delle pene*. France was slow to abolish torture. She did not follow the example of Tuscany in completely rejecting the death penalty. She made no progress towards a new codification. She maintained a cruel prison system. There are many reasons for this. They

[1] *Ibid.* p. 407.

[2] Diderot, *Œuvres politiques*, edited by Paul Vernière, Paris, 1963, p. 395, *Observations sur le Nakaz*, para. lxii.

[3] *Ibid.* p. 398.

should be sought in the power of the parliaments, and in the political importance they were gaining in those years as an autonomous and opposing force. Evidently they should also be sought in the growing social threat from the plebeian and peasant elements, the beggars and brigands in France at the close of the *ancien régime.* Modern historians, from Georges Lefebvre to George Rudé, have emphasized this social and political explanation. They have described to us in ever greater detail the situations of the classes and groups in the country and in the city. These historians start from a sociological conception and succeed in discovering a reality which Diderot had guessed at; they succeed in using calculation just where Diderot had thought it should be used.[1] But now that we know all these figures so well, we must still return to the problem of whether that delay in the transformation of France did not also derive, at least to a certain extent, from a distrust of partial reforms, from the lesser importance attributed to the problems of the penal code, from the conviction which finally prevailed among the *philosophes* that only a complete and integral transformation of society would make possible the improvements advocated by Beccaria.

Diderot had already appeared to yield on a decisive point. He had written about a man who had been killed by one of the many social causes, from prostitution to casualties under the wheels of coaches: 'peut être un fripon ou un homme de bien, au lieu que celui qui tombe sous le glaive de la justice est au moins un homme suspect, presque toujours un homme convaincu, et dont le retour à la probité est désespéré'.[2] Thus, he overcame the obstacle, which Beccaria had considered insurmountable, to every capital punishment, whether the victim was innocent or guilty, good or bad. In the end, Diderot had given up all hope of saving those who had embarked on a life of crime. Beccaria believed that it was not the social categories which should guide justice, nor the moral ones, whatever they were. It was rather the pure and simple desire not to kill, not to continue the struggles of

[1] Of Georges Lefebvre's works, one has only to recall, *Les paysans du Nord pendant la Révolution française*, Lille (1924) and Bari (1924), *La Grande peur, 1789*, Paris (1932). These and the other, numerous, works by him and by his school, have enlarged our knowledge of French society during the decline of the *ancien régime.* Of George Rudé, see especially *The crowd in history. 1730–1848*, New York–London, 1964.

[2] Diderot, *Œuvres complètes*, edited by J. Assézat, vol. IV, Paris, 1875, pp. 60 ff.

the state of nature, not, in such a way, to destroy the very base of human society as he conceived it.

The abandonment of the central conception of Beccaria seems to have given rise among the Parisian *philosophes* to a sort of rush of paradoxes, to have given a free rein to their social fantasy. For example, traditionally one attributes to Morellet the following idea which might more obviously be attributed to Diderot: to make true slaves of the convicts who, as slaves, would be 'employés à la propagation du genre humain'. Their children would be 'élevés avec soin dans des lieux destinés à cela'. Apart from the economic advantage of adding to the labour force, this would also have the scientific advantage of demonstrating the falsity of the 'préjugé de la transmissibilité des vices'. The unrestrained philosopher who reasoned thus even thought about how these convicts could be punished in their function as reproducers: 'attacher plus ou moins à l'acte même du plaisir, à la douceur de devenir pères, l'humiliation et l'amertume'.[1]

This is one of the most paradoxical and strange aspects of all the eighteenth-century casuistry in the various forms the repression of crime should take, once torture and the death penalty had been discarded. One might also be tempted to assert that the punitory imagination, which for centuries had concerned itself with inventing ever more refined torments, new wheels and pincers, more complex and spectacular ways of dismembering delinquents, now flowed along the channels which the new utilitarianism, the new social calculation, the new conception of the relationship between individual and society seemed imperiously to indicate. Maupertuis had already proposed making use of convicts for medical experiments, and the idea was repeated to Beccaria himself by the greatest Piedmontese economist of the eighteenth century, Giambattista Vasco.[2] The organization of forced labour in such a way as to make it more effective and useful was the favourite topic of such speculations. As we have seen the Tuscan code was the first to abolish the death penalty completely. The articles of the law of 1786 regarding hard labour make curious read-

[1] Beccaria, *Dei delitti e delle pene*, p. 390.

[2] Pierre-Louis Moreau de Maupertuis, *Lettre sur le progrès des sciences* (1752), in *Œuvres*, Lyon, 1756, para. ii, *Utilité du supplice des criminels*, and Beccaria, *Dei delitti e delle pene*, pp. 211 ff., letter from Giambattista Vasco to Beccaria, dated 31 January 1768.

ing.[1] In every corner of Europe, people strove to organize convicts according to Beccaria's teaching, to make them more useful to society and to themselves. All the discussions about lazarets and prisons, from Howard to Bentham, in the last years of the eighteenth century, constitute another typical meeting point of an authentic and profound Enlightenment philanthropy, a new economic calculation, and, something more disturbing, an ancient cruelty which was assuming new and more rational forms.

There was no lack in France of people ready to take up and develop the arguments Facchinei had begun against the punishments which were to take the place of the death penalty and against Beccaria's proposal of hard labour. The *Journal œconomique*, of April 1770, published a *Fragment d'une lettre de M. Linguet à l'auteur du Traité des délits et des peines*. The author seemed to see the convicts before his eyes. 'Il faut des gardes, à vos prisonniers, il faut des aliments, nourissez-les mal, en les accablant de fatigues, ils périront bientôt; il n'y aura de changé que le nom et l'appareil de la peine, car ce sera toujours vous qui les aurez tués.' Was hard labour only a hypocritical evasion for those who refused to look the death penalty in the face? This last, and this alone, was the *extrema ratio*. Only the gallows could stop the rich and the aristocracy from exercising 'leur droit de commettre des crimes sans inquiétude...Votre douceur seroit l'appas du crîme. Il ne resteroit à la chaîne que les criminels les plus indigents, les plus dépourvus de ressources et par conséquent les plus excusables suivant vos principes.'[2] The real problem did not concern the gallows or hard labour, but a society divided into rich and poor, the oppressed and the oppressors. As long as this situation existed, premature humanitarianism and lenience favoured the rich and the powerful. The poor and the oppressed still needed protection. As Linguet explained in the many other works he published in these years, this could only come from a strong, and even despotic, central power.

The discussion of hard labour spread throughout Europe, and took the form of an even harder and more pitiless calculation of the utilization of the labour of the convicts. On the other hand, Ščerbatov, in Russia, reminded legislators of their duty not to mask under the guise

[1] Beccaria, *Dei delitti e delle pene*, pp. 258 ff.

[2] Beccaria, *Dei delitti e delle pene*, p. 454, taken from the *Journal œconomique*, April 1770, pp. 171 ff., and from the *Mercure de France*, July 1770, pp. 139 ff.

of hard labour or the punishment of the knout, a capital execution much worse than the one which had been formally abolished.[1] The debate brought to everyone's attention facts and problems which were bound to arise if one tried to act on the teaching of *Dei delitti e delle pene.*

Giuseppe Gorani tried to reply to Linguet, taking Montesquieu as his starting point. He based his arguments on the idea that tolerance and a just sense of balance in punishment would, in the end, reduce the number and cruelty of crimes. A mild punishment was the best means of prevention. A less intimidating justice would face a decreasing number of criminals. In the last analysis, the reforms would improve society.[2]

But the idea that social inequality and injustice made such hopes vain always eventually dominated this debate. It overruled different opinions. No one said it more energetically than Mably in his work *De la législation ou principes des lois*, published in 1776, the year of the fall of Turgot, the decisive year for the fate of the Enlightenment reforms in France.[3] The heart of his book consists of a dialogue between 'deux hommes d'un mérite rare, l'un suédois et l'autre anglois'. Both were distinguished 'dans les assemblées de leurs pays'. The Englishman represented British patriotism and philanthropy. The Swede sustained the principles of equality and the most austere and rigid political morality. Both began from the premise that 'la nature invitoit les hommes à la communauté des biens', but that there were very grave obstacles in the way of a 'rétablissement de l'égalité'. When a society which had been created to be communist did not succeed in becoming so, everything drove men to the tragic necessity of setting up harsh penal laws and inflicting the most terrible punishments on their fellows. 'Voilà ce que c'est d'avoir établi cette

[1] See especially, Leon Radzinowicz, *A history of criminal law and its administration from 1750*, vol. I, *The movement for reform*, London, 1948; James Heath, *Eighteenth-century penal theory*, Oxford, 1963; Gustav Radbruch, *Elegantiae juris criminalis, Vierzehn Studien zur Geschichte des Strafrechts*, Basel, 1950; M. M. Ščerbatov, *Sočinenija*, edited by I. P. Chruščov, St Petersburg, 1898, vol. I, pp. 427 ff.

[2] Beccaria, *Dei delitti e delle pene*, pp. 458 ff., taken from Giuseppe Gorani, *Il vero dispotismo*, London (Geneva), 1770, vol. II, p. 227.

[3] Beccaria, *Dei delitti e delle pene*, pp. 469 ff., taken from Gabriel Bonnot de Mably, *De la législation ou principes des lois*, Amsterdam, 1776, vol. II, pp. 92 ff., book III, chap. IV, 'Que le législateur doit faire aimer ses lois. Les châtimens doivent être doux. Du pouvoir des bonnes mœurs pour attacher les citoyens au gouvernement.'

propriété qui a fait naître tant de vices dans le monde et qui force presque le législateur à être barbare. Il est vraisemblable que si les hommes avoient vécu dans cette heureuse communauté de biens que je regretterai éternellement, leurs passions sages, prudentes et tranquilles, sans effort, n'auroient pas eu besoin d'être réprimées par cette sévérité terrible dont la justice est aujourd'hui obligée de s'armer.' But by now, nothing could be done: utopia had passed. Only hard realism and the acceptance of the laws of an unjust society remained. Every hope of reform was an illusion, every indulgence of the 'beaux sentiments d'humanité', every rejection of the death penalty, every attempt to put other punishments in its place, brought to mind 'cette cruauté sublime de Tibère qui ne faisoit mourir ses ennemis que quand il avoit épuisé tous les moyens de les tourmenter'. Why torture people with hard labour? Why oblige guards to become monsters? Why hope that the convicts would be humiliated and serve as an example to others? On the contrary, they maintained their dignity only by being proud of their knavery. 'Il n'y a pas quinze jours que je rencontrai une bande de malheureux qu'on envoyoit aux galères...Ils chantoient de toute leur force...' It was better to accept the indestructible necessity of the right to punish when man was not able to re-establish communism. It was better not to close one's eyes before the scaffold.

Thus the men of the 1770s and 1780s in France were preparing for the revolution. They did so in many different ways. It would be worthwhile to follow those of Brissot de Warville and of Condorcet, for example. Both took part in an impassioned discussion of Beccaria's ideas.[1] One only has to open the *Encyclopédie méthodique* at the volume on the *Économie politique* published in 1778, to sense their supreme overwhelming weariness when confronted by reform, their scepticism and the now triumphant realism, immediately before ideas of reform and utopia began a new cycle in France and Europe.

[1] Beccaria, *Dei delitti e delle pene*, pp. 500 ff., see especially, by Brissot de Warville the *Recherches philosophiques sur le droit de propriété et sur le vol, considérés dans la nature et dans la société*, Chartres (1780) and the *Théorie des lois criminelles*, Berlin (1781) and the letter of Condorcet to Frederick of 2 May with the replies of the king of Prussia of 14 May and 29 June 1785, in *Œuvres*, edited by A. Condorcet O'Connor and F. Arago, Paris, 1847–9, pp. 303 ff.

V

THE CHRONOLOGY AND GEOGRAPHY OF THE ENLIGHTENMENT

A POLITICAL PROBLEM, namely the republican tradition, and a judicial and moral problem, the right to punish, have led us to a point where the path divides in a thousand ways, and we are led on to the Enlightenment in all its many aspects. Fortunately there is no lack of scholars ready to undertake such an enterprise. Our final task, however, must be to look at the Europe of the Enlightenment as a whole. We must try to feel its rhythm and define its extent. I attempted something similar in a report to the historians' Congress held at Stockholm in 1960.[1] Perhaps it will be useful here to voice my doubts and second thoughts, the additions and corrections stimulated by the numerous studies of the last decade, and also my own researches, especially on eighteenth-century Italy.

The many essays on the economic history of the eighteenth century still provide a very uneven picture, which varies from region to region and country to country, in this period. We know about certain aspects very well, while many others remain obscure. But, even though our information is fragmentary, or even sometimes non-existent, I believe we can no longer avoid the question which every student of the eighteenth century must ask himself. How far is the general trend of the French economy described by Labrousse valid also for the rest of the continent?[2] A period of expansion in the first quarter of the century is followed by the depression of the 1730s. The economy recovers in the 1740s, and a new period of expansion lasts until about 1770. This is followed by a period of ups and downs which leads on to the years of the revolution. It is not easy to recognize such a trend outside France. In countries such as Italy or Germany, which are

[1] F. Venturi, *L'illuminismo nel Settecento europeo* in *XIe Congrès international des sciences historiques. Rapports*, IV, *Histoire moderne*, Göteborg–Stockholm–Uppsala, 1960, pp. 106 ff.

[2] C. E. Labrousse, *Esquisse du mouvement des prix et des revenus en France au XVIIIe siècle*, Paris, 1932, and G. Lefebvre, 'Le mouvement des prix et les origines de la Révolution française', in *Annales d'histoire économique et sociale*, IX, 1937, pp. 139 ff.

politically broken up into small pieces, the smallness of the local markets tends to obscure the general trends of the economy. In other countries, such as those of eastern Europe, the continuance of serfdom gives the whole economy a different form, as the recent studies by Witold Kula have confirmed.[1] In England the beginning of the industrial revolution also profoundly transforms the situation.[2] And so we could go on for the most diverse countries. Yet, in spite of everything, one can hardly fail to recognize a common rhythm among all the local differences. Every time one looks at Labrousse's price curve for wheat in France; every time one notes the increase in the population of eighteenth-century Europe, it is clear that all society, and not just the movement of ideas and politics, is expanding at the beginning of the century, reaches a crisis in the thirties and reaches its peak in the fifties and sixties, while the last twenty-five years of the century witness a period of profound disturbance. It is the curve of the eighteenth century, and also of the Enlightenment.

Yet, although this is true, it is equally true that the rhythm varies according to local conditions. There is progress and delay, immobility and abrupt advances. Let us consider the thirties and forties when the trend was reversed, and look at what happened in the various countries. In the Iberian peninsula, the economists restate the ideas and programmes that had been formulated in the years immediately after the war of the Spanish succession. At that time the conditions imposed by the Treaty of Utrecht had provoked not only an attempt to regain what had been lost, but also a movement towards internal reform. The work by Uztáriz, first published in 1724, was reprinted and much more widely read in 1742.[3] As Richard Herr adds in his *The eighteenth century revolution in Spain*, 'two other writers, Bernardo de Ulloa, and the Minister of Finance, José del Campillo y Cossio joined Uztáriz about 1740 in urging the need to increase Spain's manufactures, commerce, and population'.[4] Beside the rationalism of

[1] W. Kula, *Teoria economica del sistema feudale. Proposta d'un modello*, Turin, 1970.

[2] Peter Mathias, *The first industrial nation. An economic history of Britain, 1700–1914*, London, 1969.

[3] Gerónimo de Uztáriz, *Théorica y práctica de comercio y de marina*, Madrid, 1724, 1742, 1757. Cf. J. Hamilton, *The Mercantilism of Gerónimo de Uztáriz: a reëxamination*, in *Economics, Sociology, and the Modern World*, edited by Norman E. Himes, Cambridge, Mass., 1935, pp. 111 ff.

[4] Richard Herr, *The eighteenth century revolution in Spain*, Princeton, 1958, p. 48.

Fejoo and the judicial theories of Macanaz, there was also a desire for economic reform.[1] In Italy, the thirties seem to be the lowest point of the political, economic and intellectual crisis throughout the country. Giannone was in prison. Radicati died in exile. Vittorio Amedeo II's zeal for reform was dwindling into insignificance in Turin. The Austrian vice-realm was becoming weaker and weaker in Naples. Papal policies had never seemed so fragile. Nevertheless, in spite of the war of the Austrian succession between 1740 and 1748, the signs of a recovery are evident. The great elderly scholars, Muratori and Maffei, increasingly turn their attention to the problem of society. They discuss usury, the rhythm of work and public welfare. Sallustio Bandini opens the way to the Tuscan free-traders. Carlantonio Broggia, in 1743, writes the chief treatise on economics, published in Italy before *Della Moneta* by Galiani (1751).[2] In Austria and in Prussia, 1740 marks the beginning of a new epoch, with the advent of Maria Theresa and Frederick II.[3] In France, in the forties, new intellectual activity develops, writings against religion multiply and some are even printed. Through the works of Bacon, Shaftesbury and Berkeley, it is English thought which flows into France. The group of young men who were to create the *Encyclopédie* was rapidly forming. It was these men—Diderot and Rousseau, La Mettrie and d'Holbach, d'Alembert and Raynal, Mably and Condillac—who were to set the tone of the whole of French encyclopaedism. The *Pensées philosophiques* by Diderot were written in 1746. *L'esprit des lois*, which brings one age to a close and begins another, dates from 1748.[4]

[1] Jean Sarrailh, *L'Espagne éclairée de la seconde moitié du XVIIIè siècle*, Paris, 1954, and J. Vicens Vives, *Manual de historia económica de España*, Barcelona, 1959.

[2] F. Venturi, *Settecento riformatore*.

[3] Eduard Winter, *Der Josefinismus und seine Geschichte. Beiträge zur Geistesgeschichte Oesterreichs. 1740–1848*, Brünn–Munich–Vienna, 1943 and Manfred Schlenke, *England und das friderizianische Preussen. 1740–1763. Ein Beitrag zum Verhältnis von Politik und öffentlicher Meinung im England des 18. Jahrhunderts*, Munich, 1963. Werner Krauss, *Studien zur deutschen und französischen Aufklärung*, Berlin, 1963.

[4] Ira O. Wade, *The clandestine organization and diffusion of philosophic ideas in France from 1700 to 1750*, Princeton, 1938; F. Venturi, *Jeunesse de Diderot. De 1713 à 1753*, Paris, 1939; Paul Vernière, *Spinoza et la pensée française avant la Révolution*, Paris, 1954; F. Venturi, *Le origini dell'Enciclopedia*, Turin, 1963; J. Th. de Booy, *Histoire d'un manuscrit de Diderot: 'La promenade du sceptique'*, Frankfurt-am-Main, 1964; John Lough, *Essays on the 'Encyclopédie' of Diderot and d'Alembert*, Oxford, 1968; *A critical bibliography of French literature*, vol. IV. *The eighteenth century. Supplement*, edited by Richard A. Brooks, Syracuse, 1968.

The general trend seems clear. But have we the right to place such diverse and disparate facts side by side? Aren't the local differences more important than the similarities? If we take a closer look, if we examine in detail the situations in Spain, Italy, Vienna, Berlin and Paris, we must conclude that the links between them and many other similar elements were more numerous and more substantial than might seem at first sight; that the circulation of ideas was more effective than we might have suspected, that hopes and expectations were turned in the same direction, and that, effectively, we are witnessing the emergence of Enlightened Europe. We are no longer confronted by the crisis of the European conscience of the beginning of the century; nor by a continuation of the disputes between Jansenists and Molinists, between Laxists and Rigorists, Deists and anti-Deists and Curialists, among the various schools deriving from Cartesian rationalism or the different currents of natural law. Something new was being born. We are passing from the *Frühaufklärung* to the *Aufklärung*.[1] Religious and moral problems were giving way to political and social ones. Legal problems were giving way to economic ones. Philosophic system gives place to the experimentation and Pyrrhonism to a new faith in nature.

Paris was of central importance in the years in which the *Encyclopédie* was under preparation. There was already a cosmopolitan air, even if it was due to obscure German professors, such as Sellius, and equally unknown English writers, such as John Mills. On the other hand, even Diderot and Rousseau were completely unknown at the beginning of the forties. It was a new generation. They formed a new social milieu, very different from that of Fontenelle, Montesquieu, or Voltaire, to name only the men who dominated the intellectual horizons of France at that time. This world was extraordinarily alive with writers, translators and people making a living with their pen and existing for their own ideas. Voltaire tried to approach the court and the academy. He even succeeded in establishing a surprising *modus vivendi* with Pope Benedict XIV himself. In these years, Montesquieu negotiated and discussed with church and state, almost as if he were a political force. Sometimes he conceded and sometimes

[1] Eduard Winter, *Frühaufklärung. Der Kampf gegen den Konfessionalismus in Mittel- und Osteuropa und die deutsch-slawische Begegnung*, Berlin, 1966.

he did not, according to the circumstances. He was the real arbiter and lord of political thought of his time. He remained detached and brilliant. At this very time the group of young encyclopaedists was closely watched by the police. It was threatened by imprisonment in the castle of Vincennes, as happened to Diderot in 1749 at the time of a general repression of heterodox elements when the country was at last emerging from the war. These young men must constantly have struggled with the censorship, with the corporative rules of the *librairie*, and even with their own families and environment. There was extraordinary freedom within the group. Diderot inspired it. D'Alembert followed with some misgivings. Rousseau interpreted in his own way the ideas and enthusiasms of the group. They all rejected any protection for the nascent *Encyclopédie*, just as they rejected all rigid internal organization. They did not depend on the state. They were not an academy. They were a group of free philosophers.

Throughout Europe, the words and actions of the encyclopaedists in Paris at the end of the forties and the beginning of the fifties, between the preparation and the first critical point of the *Encyclopédie* in 1752, were followed with rapidly increasing interest and curiosity. In Tuscany, the *Giornale dei letterati pubblicato in Firenze* from 1747 on, provides excellent information on the *Encyclopédie*. One can find in it information which has been neglected even by current students of the movement. In Germany, they soon became aware of the irreligious upheaval in Paris, and a great deal of discussion and confutation took place. The relationships with England, with those who were adding supplements to Ephraim Chambers's *Cyclopaedia* and with those who were translating and expanding this work in Paris, became more and more intense. The letters of John Mills to Thomas Birch, preserved in the British Museum, are particularly curious in this respect. They underline, among other things, the entire difference between the France of Louis XV and England in those years. Confronted by the will of the chancellor, said John Mills on 21 June 1745, 'in this country, far different in that respect from England, one is forced to obey'.[1]

However great this interest in what was being thought and said in Paris, both in France and elsewhere (and there is no lack of examples),

[1] F. Venturi, *Le origini dell'Enciclopedia*, p. 28.

it is still evident that the liberty and intellectual emancipation reigning in the group of the young *philosophes* was too great, too intense to be assimilated by Europe in the middle of the eighteenth century. There are many refutations of their works, the editions and translations relatively few, not only of the *Lettre sur les aveugles*, or of the *Pensées philosophiques* by Diderot, but also of d'Alembert's admirable work *Essai sur la société des gens de lettres et des grands, sur la réputation, sur les mécènes et sur les récompenses littéraires*, published in 1753. This book is an admirable code and guide for the free writer. It can be used as a gauge for measuring the differences between the behaviour of intellectuals in Paris and intellectuals in the other European centres at the time. One sees the superior independence, dignity and effectiveness of the nascent intelligentsia of the Enlightenment.[1] Such a comparison would also lead one to the conclusion that the French group was isolated, unique in Europe.

Yet it is the *Encyclopédie* which bridges the gaps between the thought of the Parisian group and the rest of Europe. The very fact that it was a dictionary of the sciences and the arts made the diffusion of the new ideas possible, even when they certainly could not have arrived independently. Technical culture was linked to the conceptions which Diderot had been forming of labour, machines, the relationship between philosophy and everyday life, between ideas and society. Science was not merely expounded. From the *Discours préliminaire* to the articles on methodology by d'Alembert, it was consistently seen in historical perspective of the formation and triumph of modern civilization. Politics and law were constantly under discussion, as part of the much larger philosophical and moral problems which Diderot and his collaborators repeatedly set before their readers. So what does it matter if prudence and censorship obliged the encyclopaedists to be very cautious on the topic of religion? The old objection that the great dictionary was not really a weapon of war, for example, the observation made by Daniel Mornet that if one considers the *Encyclopédie* closely, it is seen to be much more anodyne and even more orthodox than the legend claims, misses the mark. It was a question of changing people's ways of thinking, as Diderot said. To do this, half way through the century, a new exposition of the relationship

[1] R. Grimsley, *Jean d'Alembert. 1717–1783*, Oxford, 1963.

between art and letters, between science and society, arranged alphabetically, was more effective than a pamphlet of more direct religious or political polemic. Or rather, both were necessary, as Diderot well knew, when he published his *Pensées sur l'interprétation de la nature* at the time when the large tomes of the *Encyclopédie* were beginning to appear again after the crisis of 1752.

This is confirmed by a comparison between the situation in France and the rest of Europe. Diderot's pamphlet was the essence of that encyclopaedic spirit which was soon to be appreciated and assimilated in Italy, Spain, England and in Germany.[1] The first Italian translator of the *Discours préliminaire* was the doge of Genoa, Agostino Lomellini.[2] The Swiss and English printers turned out a large number of dictionaries of the sciences and of the arts. In a decade, the Enlightenment and the *Encyclopédie* almost coincided. The history of these events has become increasingly better known, thanks to the multiplication of works on the *rayonnement* of the work of Diderot and d'Alembert.

There is, however, one aspect which is still worth a moment of our attention because, in contrast with the others, it does not seem to me to have been studied closely enough. How far did the *Encyclopédie* promote and assist the passage from politics and law to economics, which is one of the general and fundamental trends in the forties and fifties in England, as in Spain, Italy and Austria? It did more than is generally assumed, and from the very beginning. The key figure in the early years is François Véron de Forbonnois who wrote the articles on political economy in the *Encyclopédie*, and later collected and published them under the name of *Élémens du commerce* in 1754.[3] These pages help us better than anything else to understand the modification of the economic climate of opinion after the middle of the century, at the very time when the need for a science of economics

[1] Association internationale des études françaises, *Cahiers*, vol. II, *L'Encyclopédie et son rayonnement à l'étranger*, Paris, 1952; Roland Mortier, *Diderot en Allemagne. 1750–1850*, Paris, 1954 (a revised and enlarged German translation will soon be published).

[2] Salvatore Rotta, 'Documenti per la storia dell'illuminismo a Genova. Lettere di Agostino Lomellini a Paolo Frisi' in *Miscellanea di storia ligure*, vol. I, Genoa, 1958, pp. 189 ff.

[3] Cf. the article, insufficient though it may, be by Christian Morrison, *La place de Forbonnais dans la pensée économique* in Christian Morrison and Robert Goffin, *Questions financières aux XVIIIe et XIXe siècles*, Paris, 1967.

becomes more and more urgent. Forbonnois was accompanied by a group of people, his friends and, in some cases, his relatives, such as Herbert, Butel-Dumont and Plumard de Dangueil, who, encouraged and helped by Vincent de Gournay, published an impressive number of books and translations in the fifties, and made France the centre of the most lively discussions of the subject in Europe at that time.[1] In a particularly important field, they performed the same functions as the encyclopaedists. They were no longer isolated as Melon and Dutot were in the thirties and forties. They were already a group with a recognizable body of theory. From this point of view, they also bridged the gap between the economists of the first half of the century and the physiocrats who, in the sixties, formed such a compact movement that contemporaries described them as a sect. Their political importance can immediately be appreciated if one opens the *Remarques sur les avantages et les désavantages de la France et de la Grande Bretagne*, which Plumard de Dangeuil published under the pseudonym of John Nickolls.[2] The comparison with Great Britain is no longer constitutional, political, religious, or cultural. It is entirely economic and social. The freedom spoken of is the freedom of trade. Equality concerns property and taxes. Justice consists of a better investment of capital and labour. It is a surprisingly fresh and impressive work. Naturally, the comparison was entirely to England's advantage. However, the parallel and comparison was not only made with England by this group of economists—who deserve a closer examination rather than merely being labelled as late mercantilists. England remained their great model. It was these people who made known the writings of Davenant, Joshua Gee, Charles King and John Cary. But they turned their attention with equal interest towards Spain: they re-opened the discussion on the causes of its decadence; Forbonnois proposed new financial policies; Vincent de Gournay lived there for a long period. The works of Uztáriz and Ulloa appeared in French translations with commentaries. They did something similar for Italy, although on a smaller scale. Once more, it was Forbonnois who wrote the most interesting commentary on the new land register drawn up in the fifties by Pompeo Neri in Austrian Lombardy. Plumard de Dangueil visited Antonio Genovesi in Naples,

[1] Furio Diaz, *Filosofia e politica nel Settecento francese*.

[2] Leyden, 1754.

and discussed with him the fundamental problems of the economy of southern Italy. Spain and Italy willingly acknowledged their debt. Their works were translated and widely discussed. Antonio Genovesi and Pietro Verri started from them.[1] Such a wide diffusion requires an explanation which goes beyond personal contacts and intellectual fashions. It seems clear that it was this late mercantilism itself, if we wish to call it that, which was best suited to countries other than France and England. They were aware of their own situation through the comparison with richer and more active countries, and looked to the culture of the *Encyclopédie* for the means with which to overthrow the decadence they were becoming more and more acutely conscious of. In fact, when Quesnay began writing in the *Encyclopédie*, and establishing the base of physiocracy with the articles *Fermiers* and *Grains* in volumes VI and VII of 1756 and 1757, the penetration of the new ideas was more difficult and slow, not only in France, but especially beyond her frontiers. The Marquis Victor Riqueti de Mirabeau managed to move on from Cantillon to Quesnay and his work certainly had a notable success everywhere in Europe where his books *L'ami des hommes* and the *Théorie de l'impôt* were widely read.[2] But a closer examination seems to reveal that these books were welcomed for what was familiar in them, not for what was new, for their arguments against absolutism rather than their physiocratic ideas. The penetration of the *Tableau*, and of Quesnay's ideas in general was slow and difficult in Germany and in Italy, in Poland and in Spain. It took place only at the end of the sixties, and more especially in the seventies. This was as true of Baden as it was of Lombardy. Even in cases such as Tuscany, where, from 1766, one might assume that his ideas had a direct influence on the tariff policies of Pietro Leopoldo, very often one is witnessing a renewal of a local free-trade movement, blended with the French polemics of the fifties in favour of free-trade. This has been demonstrated in a monograph on Francesco Gianni by Furio Diaz, the Italian scholar who has done the most work on these questions.[3] It should be pointed out that the passage from late

[1] F. Venturi, *Settecento riformatore*.

[2] Victor Riqueti de Mirabeau, *L'ami des hommes ou Traité de la population*, Avignon, 1756; *idem*, *Théorie de l'impôt*, The Hague, 1760.

[3] Carl Friedrich von Baden, *Brieflicher Verkehr mit Mirabeau und Du Pont*, edited by Carl Knies, Heidelberg, 1892; Ambroise Jobert, *Magnats polonais et physiocrates*

mercantilism to physiocracy is one of those topics which has been studied country by country (in Poland, Italy and Germany) while no attempt has been made to find a general European rhythm by studying the local situations in relation to a significant and more general view.

Thus, the diffusion of the economic ideas from Paris is yet another example of that differentiated rhythm we can perceive in the first reactions to the *Encyclopédie* in the 1750s. Although great interest was shown, although the volumes which appeared between the first and second crises of the great dictionary, between 1752 and 1759, were a great stimulus, one often gains the impression that Paris was ten years ahead of the other countries. Spain was passing through a crisis which was not only dynastic, while waiting for the arrival of Charles III from Naples, in 1759. Italy seemed to withdraw into herself after the strain of the post-war period. Lombardy welcomed reform, but everywhere else the efforts and attempts were increasingly difficult and slow. At Vienna, the Empire took the first step forward with the changes achieved by Haugwitz: but intellectual life stagnated in the fifties and the horizon was soon dominated by the renewal of war. The situation in Germany varied extraordinarily from region to region, but practically everywhere, and as early as this period, views comparable to those expressed in the *Encyclopédie* found expression in the fields of arts and morality. They were of no great importance in the social, political and economic life of the country. One has only to remember the fate of Lessing to understand the phenomenon. In Prussia, the Enlightenment came from above. Absolutism and reform were so closely interwoven that very little space remained not only for groups and movements but even for individuals, as Voltaire was to find out for himself. In England, the fifties saw the publication of Hume's *Essays*.[1] Intellectual life was animated, political activity was intense, but they did not possess the characteristics of Enlightenment movements. They did not have an organization

français (1764–1774), Paris, 1941; Edward Lipiński, *De Copernic à Stanislas Leszczyński. La pensée économique et démographique en Pologne*, Paris–Warsaw, 1961; Institut national d'études démographiques, *François Quesnay et la physiocratie*, Paris, 1958; François Quesnay, *Scritti economici*, introduction by Renato Zangheri, Bologna, 1966; Furio Diaz, *Francesco Maria Gianni. Dalla burocrazia alla politica sotto Pietro Leopoldo di Toscana*, Milan–Naples, 1966.

[1] David Hume, *Essays and treatises on several subjects*, London, 1753–6.

or a rhythm of their own. So they did not operate as a new and autonomous political force, which tended to question or replace organisms inherited from the past. In eastern Europe, the reforms of the Piarists in Poland were enacted by Konarski, and the university of Cracow improved under Andrzej Stanisław Załuski. But one can see that these developments were due to the diffusion of Enlightenment thought; they were not yet the work of an autonomous movement capable of striking against any point of the Sarmatian conservatism. Only at the beginning of the sixties did the situation begin to change. A very similar state of affairs existed in Russia. Masonry gained a stronger hold. Periodicals and reviews were founded. Scientific, literary and moral discussions started up in the reign of Elisabeth. But the cultural atmosphere was still dominated by the scientific activities of Lomonosov and by the academic organization of the German scholars. The heritage of Peter still dominated Russia. Catherine's *coup d'état* in 1762 opened a new epoch, both in Russia and in Poland.

The great convergence of those who were ahead of the times, and those who were behind, of those who had shown the way, and those who had tried to follow, took place in the sixties, at a time when the men of the Enlightenment seemed to work in unison, a decisive time for the whole of Europe. It was the time when, as she descended the Volga on a boat with her friends and ministers, Catherine translated and ordered to be translated the *Belisarius* by Marmontel, among other works of the French encyclopaedists. She demanded that the constantly increasing number of books arriving from the west should be studied and translated. She herself contributed to the new journals. She encouraged the spread of masonry. In every way possible, she tried to animate the great state apparatus begun by Peter with the new ideas. As the poet, Cheraskov, said, Peter gave Russia a body, Catherine gave it a soul. In a certain sense, this was true. The *philosophes* became the soul of eighteenth-century Russia at that time.[1] In

[1] Horst Jablonowski, 'Die geistige Bewegung in Russland in der zweiten Hälfte des 18. Jahrhunderts' in *Le mouvement des idées dans les pays slaves pendant la seconde moitié du XVIIIè siècle. Atti del colloquio slavistico tenutosi ad Uppsala il 19–21 agosto 1960*, Rome, 1962, pp. 7 ff.; F. Venturi 'Quelques notes sur le rapport de Horst Jablonowski', *ibid.* pp. 26 ff.; *Svodnyj katalog russkoj knigi graždanskoj pečati XVIII veka. 1725–1800*, Moscow, 1962–6, 5 vols; Marc Raef, *Origins of the Russian intelligentsia. The eighteenth-century nobility*, New York, 1966; Paul Bourychkine,

Spain, on the other side of Europe, Charles III was beginning a process of modernization which soon met serious obstacles in the religious and other traditions of the people. Yet he succeeded, at least partially, in overcoming or circumventing them, and finally opened the way to a continuous process of reform in the Iberian peninsula. However slow and uneven it may have been, it had at last found an internal logic and a political momentum derived from European Enlightenment.[1] In Italy, this was the age of the *Accademia dei Pugni* in Milan, and of the *Lezioni di commercio* of Antonio Genovesi in Naples. The reforms in Tuscany were making headway, while a determination to change things was spreading throughout the peninsula: for example, the formation of the 'agrarian societies' in the provinces of the Venetian republic; the re-organization of Cagliari university; the attempts of Dalmazzo Francesco Vasco to get into contact with Jean-Jacques Rousseau and to collaborate with him in the Corsican rebellion; the publication at Chur in the Grisons and the work by Carlantonio Pilati, *Di una riforma d'Italia*.[2] In spite of the censorship in Austria, the *Deutsche Gesellschaft* and the first writings by Sonnenfels, such as his *Man ohne Vohurtheile*, show the relationship between Enlightenment and reform in a new light.[3] In Scotland, a great intellectual movement was about to be born while London resounded to the cry of 'Wilkes and Liberty'![4]

Everywhere, after a long preparation, it seemed that the era of the Enlightenment had arrived. It was not only the intellectuals who were in turmoil. The movement assumed very diverse forms; for example, the peasants who poured into Naples in an attempt to escape the terrible famine of 1764; the common people of Madrid who provoked the 'motín de Esquilace'; the people who followed Wilkes in London. As for the political classes, they were all in a state of change throughout Europe at the time the Seven Years' war was coming to an end. The

Bibliographie sur la franc-maçonnerie en Russie, complétée et mise au point par Tatiana Bakounine, Paris–The Hague, 1964; Paul Dukes, *Catherine the Great and the Russian nobility*, Cambridge, 1967.

[1] Besides the books mentioned on p. 182, nn. 3 and and 4 and p. 183, n. 1, cf. Robert Jones Shafer, *The economic societies in the Spanish world (1763–1821)*, Syracuse, 1958, and Marcelin Defourneaux, *Pablo Olavide ou l'afrancesado (1725–1803)*, Paris, 1959.

[2] *Illuministi italiani*, vols. III, V, VII.

[3] Robert A. Kahn, *A study in Austrian intellectual history. From late Baroque to Romanticism*, New York, 1960.

[4] George Rudé, *Wilkes and Liberty. A social study of 1763 to 1774*, Oxford, 1962.

surge of reform and ideas spread in all directions: it reached the British colonies in America and the regiments of the Guard at St Petersburg.

However diverse the problems of the various parts of Europe were, they found a common language and centre in the France of the sixties and in the extraordinary intellectual life there. It was in these years that thinkers began to reproach philosophy for its abstract quality, and yet it was this very quality which enabled the new ideas to penetrate and spread beyond national frontiers and overcome differences in social structure. It is certainly odd to see the *Contrat social* serve as a shield to conservatism in Poland, to those who rejected any reform of the golden Sarmatian liberty, or to see *Dei delitti e delle pene* become an instrument in the hands of the nobility, who found in its rejection of the death penalty and in the mildness of the punishments it advocated yet another pretext for the free exercise of their arbitrary will.[1] But this is the price which must be paid for new political and judicial ideas to be given a hearing throughout Europe. In Paris, the contrast between utopia and reform was so great that it polarized the conflicts and contrasts inside the most diverse countries around the issues posed by Rousseau and Boulanger, Voltaire and d'Holbach, Quesnay and Galiani.

If one examines the *troupeau des philosophes* closely, one sees that, in spite of the constant appeals for unity from Ferney, it was deeply divided, but that it was this internal struggle itself which inspired the search for the most varied ways of achieving a society completely liberated from religion, in which all political and economic mechanisms would be completely comprehensible, without obscurities and guided by reason. If one thinks that little more than a half century had passed since Pierre Bayle had maintained that a society of atheists was possible, one sees how far the eighteenth century had come. Now this society had come into being and was very much alive. Economically, it should function in accordance with evident laws; Quesnay had clearly described its organism; it was possible to foresee the phases of its development, as the physiocrats were insistently demonstrating.

[1] On the accusation of abstraction and its significance, see F. Venturi, 'Galiani tra enciclopedisti e fisiocrati' in *Rivista storica italiana*, 1960, no. 1, pp. 45 ff. On Poland as well as the works mentioned on p. 9, n. 1, see especially Jerzy Michalsky, 'Problem *ius agratiandi*, i kary śmierci w Polsce w latach siedemdziesiątych XVIII w.' in *Czasopismo prawno-historyczne*, vol. x, 1958, no. 2, pp. 175 ff.

Politically, the gap between what this society might be and what, in fact, it was in the last years of the reign of Louis XV was becoming more dramatic every year. Was it really necessary to follow the example of Medea, as Diderot said? Medea who 'rendit la jeunesse à son père en le dépeçant et le faisant bouillir'. It was no longer possible to accept both the stagnation and the restrictions on liberty imposed by the old regime.[1] A great model of a democratic society had appeared in 1762 with the publication of the *Contrat social*. A rationalization of all social relationships was demanded everywhere, in a thousand polemics against feudalism and against traditional legislation. The works of Nicolas-Antoine Boulanger offered a particularly effective vision of the evolution of humanity from a world of religion to a world of reason. The *Lettre* which opened the posthumous edition of his *Recherches sur l'origine du despotisme oriental* (by the way, I think Voltaire was right to attribute it to Diderot) now openly declared the candidature of the *philosophes* to guide the world.[2] 'L'esprit général qui se monte de plus en plus sur le ton de la raison et de l'humanité... le progrès des connaissances, ce fleuve immense qui grossit tous les jours...la soif pour l'instruction' now made it clear to everyone that society no longer needed to be governed 'par ces ressorts surnaturels qu'on appelle religion et révélation'. 'Les lois naturelles, sociales et civiles' were sufficient. 'La raison et la loi fondée sur la raison doivent être les uniques reines des mortels...Lors qu'une religion établie commence à pâlir et à s'éteindre devant les lumières d'un siècle éclairé, ce n'est plus qu'à cette raison qu'il faut immédiatement recourir pour maintenir la société et pour la sauver des malheurs de l'anarchie... À qui donner une telle commission si ce n'est à la philosophie? Elle ne doit pas même attendre qu'on la lui donne, elle a fait du passé l'objet de ses études, elle doit faire du futur l'objet de ses prévoyances,

[1] Diderot, *Réfutation suivie de l'ouvrage d'Helvétius intitulé L'homme*, in *Œuvres complètes*, edited by J. Assézat, vol. II, Paris, 1875, p. 276; cf. Diderot, *Mémoires pour Cathérine II*, edited by P. Vernière, Paris, 1966, pp. 20 ff., and what Helvétius wrote in his posthumous work, published in 1775, *De l'homme, de ses facultés intellectuelles et de son éducation*, Amsterdam, 1775. On the reaction of the French authorities, see: Jacques Donvez, 'Diderot, Aiguillon et Vergennes' in *Revue des sciences humaines*, (new series), no. 87, July–September 1957, pp. 287 ff. On the general problems of these years, Furio Diaz, *Filosofia e politica nel Settecento francese*.

[2] F. Venturi, 'Postille inedite di Voltaire ad alcune opere di Nicolas-Antoine Boulanger e del barone d'Holbach' in *Studi francesi*, 1958, no. 2, pp. 231 ff.

porter ses vues au plus loin et former un plan de philosophie politique ...On a dit l'Europe sauvage, l'Europe payenne, on a dit l'Europe Chrétienne, peut-être dira-t-on encore pis, mais il faut qu'on dise enfin l'Europe raisonnable.'[1] This appeal was answered by the countless publications of d'Holbach's group. The atheism they acclaimed was to confirm this 'philosophie politique'. As Baron d'Holbach himself explained, there was no longer any need of priests as the judges knew their own work well.[2] The social framework was able to survive and regulate itself without God. The philosophers asked to be allowed to act as guide.

Everywhere in Europe, one finds this pretension, this determination to lead and guide society. It was expressed in different ways in different situations. In France, it was certainly the most extreme and integral, the most utopian and revolutionary. But in France, also, it took the shape of reform, when, in 1774, Turgot became a minister. Even earlier, in August 1772, Diderot, who certainly did not like him, particularly because of his attitude during the crisis of the *Encyclopédie* of 1759, had written: 'Quand je ne suis seul et que je rêve qu'il y a pourtant encore parmi nous des hommes capables de reparer nos désastres, vous êtes un des premiers qui se présentent à ma pensée.'[3] His physiocratic friends had accused Turgot of being the enemy of all despotism; one of them said he was more republican than monarchical. Yet it was Turgot who made the only great attempt to bring about an enlightened despotism in France in the last years of the old regime.[4] Was not his the only possible policy in France at that time?

Thus, we should not be surprised to see in Milan the members of the *Accademia dei Pugni* rapidly becoming high officials in Austrian Lombardy, and carrying out fundamental reforms; nor to see Aranda,

[1] 'Lettre de l'auteur à M. *****' [Helvétius], preceding the *Recherches sur l'origine du despotisme oriental. Ouvrage posthume de Mr. B.I.D.P.E.C.* (Boulanger, ingénieur des ponts et chaussées) (Geneva), 1761, pp. iii ff.

[2] *Le Christianisme dévoilé, ou examen des principes et des effets de la religion chrétienne,* (Nancy?), 1767, *Lettre de l'auteur à Monsieur* ***. In vain Voltaire asserted that religion was necessary for the common people: 'C'est la loi qui contient les gens du peuple et quand un insensé leur diroit de voler ou d'assassiner, le gibet les avertiroit de n'en rien faire', replied d'Holbach.

[3] Georges Dulac, 'Une lettre de Diderot à Turgot' in *Studi francesi,* no. 36, September–December 1968, pp. 454 ff., letter dated 9 August 1772.

[4] Douglas Dakin, *Turgot and the 'Ancien régime' in France,* London, 1939.

Campomanes, Olavide and Jovellanos transform themselves into the governing class of the Spain of Charles III; nor to see the Polish landowners change into reformers and the government of Catherine II appeal to the Legislative Commission. We should not be surprised either that Leipzig University, at the time of Hommel, became a centre of active reforms, while other German territories, such as Baden, fell under the sway of physiocracy. At Genoa Agostino Lomellini was doge for two years, the translator and friend of d'Alembert. Power and philosophy seek each other, converge and diverge, according to the circumstances. Their struggles and agreements dominated republican Europe, just as they dominated monarchical Europe. They ruled over the Mediterranean, just as they ruled over eastern and central Europe.

Only one country was absent from this array of 'Enlightened' thinkers in the sixties and seventies, and that was England. That the very country which was moving towards the industrial revolution should be the only one in which the organization of the Enlightenment did not exist, should suffice in itself to call in question the oft-repeated Marxist interpretation of the Enlightenment as the ideology of the bourgeoisie. Nor can one reply that the bourgeois revolution had taken place in England a century before, because the economic historians explain to us that the internal changes which took place in England during the eighteenth century were essential. The fact remains that no 'parti des philosophes' was formed in London, and so could not claim to guide society. The struggles which did take place (one has only to recall 'Wilkes and liberty') are not those of a nascent intelligentsia. Even the English giant of the Enlightenment, Gibbon, was not only closely linked with continental culture but remained an isolated figure in his own country, a solitary figure. Nor can the resumption of the tradition of the commonwealthmen or persons such as Thomas Hollis fill this gap, however interesting they may be. They are curious and significant for the very reason that they seem to take the place of something which is missing. English radicalism, too, was born around 1764, but it exhibited very different characteristics from the philosophy of the continent. One has to wait until the eighties and nineties to find men such as Bentham, Price, Godwin and Paine. In England the rhythm was different.

I believe that the most useful way of understanding this situation is to look to the north of the British Isles, to Scotland. There, on the contrary, we find all the essential elements of an Enlightenment. Indeed, in the 1770s, it became one of the most advanced countries, in economic and historiographical terms, in the European movement. One need only recall the importance Scottish culture rapidly acquired in Paris, Naples, in Koenigsberg and in Moscow. We are still waiting for a comprehensive study of the Scottish Enlightenment. This is one of the most necessary pieces of research in the field of eighteenth-century European history.[1] It is tempting to observe that the Enlightenment was born and organized in those places where the contact between a backward world and a modern one was chronologically more abrupt, and geographically closer. It was the difference between traditional Scotland and the Glasgow and Edinburgh of the eighteenth century which created groups and societies similar to the patriotic ones of the continent, which concentrated attention on the economy and society and which posed once again all the problems of the relations between utilitarian philosophy and new policies. It was the contrast with the traditional ruling classes which gave rise to a new intelligentsia, conscious of its own function and strength. If looked at from Milan or Paris, Scotland in the sixties and seventies seems a familiar land, however great the originality and vitality of its intellectual life. Ferguson and Millar are of the same world as Filangieri and Condorcet. Dr Johnson is a native English god.

The structure of English politics certainly carries great weight in determining these similar differences. The very fact that it has been considered useful to study it in complete isolation from any ideological context, even dispensing with the labels of Whig and Tory, and with any intellectual scheme, is significant. Even if we consider Sir Lewis Namier from the point of view of the continent in the eighteenth century, he still has a lot to teach us, if only through the extraordinary

[1] Cf., among the latest and most stimulating studies, Duncan Forbes, 'Scientific Whiggism. Adam Smith and John Millar' in *Cambridge Journal*, vol. III, 1954, pp. 643 ff.; William C. Lehmann, *John Millar of Glasgow, 1735–1801. His life and his contribution to sociological analysis*, Cambridge, 1960; Adam Ferguson, *An essay on the history of civil society. 1767*, edited by Duncan Forbes, Edinburgh, 1966; A. J. Youngson, *The making of classical Edinburgh*, Edinburgh, 1968.

energy with which he has been true to his method and approach. But I am sure it will be agreed that it would be very difficult to write a history of the sixties and seventies in France and refrain from examining the links with the physiocrats and anti-physiocrats of Turgot and Necker, or a history of Milan without describing the contacts between Beccaria or Verri and the world of the Parisian encyclopaedists. Even a book like Lüthy's, which has attempted to rebuild the structure of the Protestant bank, ends by giving a very intelligent and stimulating interpretation of the ideas of physiocracy.[1] Even in those regions, such as Poland or Russia, where the Enlightenment might, mistakenly, seem only a fashion, an ornament, or mere propaganda, it soon reveals itself as firmly rooted, as Jean Fabre's book has shown.[2] If one attempts to avoid this truth, the whole picture is distorted, as happened to Lortholary.[3]

Sometimes, as I read and re-read the writings of Sir Lewis Namier, I have found myself thinking that this method, on the continent, is best suited for analysing the compact world, apparently so uniform yet full of contrasts, of the patriciates of the ancient Italian republics or, more generally, the nobilities of aristocratic states. I do not wish to imply that the Enlightenment did not penetrate into Venice, for example. On the contrary, the new thought was very diffused, as the recent studies by Berengo and by Torcellan have shown.[4] But it did not succeed in producing a movement which influenced those states deeply. Frequently it remained a cultural rather than a political force. This aspect of its role reminds one of England, where the situation was very different, but where the last decades of the eighteenth century also passed without political reform being able to get under way. Nor did those states experience the conflicts and irreparable damage suffered by France. England in the age of the Enlightenment was really an exception, and its political structure is not the least important element in explaining this fact.

[1] H. Lüthy, *La banque protestante en France*, Paris, 1959–61.

[2] Jean Fabre, *Stanislas-Auguste Poniatowski et l'Europe des lumières*.

[3] Albert Lortholary, *Le mirage russe en France au XVIIIe siècle*, Paris, 1951.

[4] Marino Berengo, *La società veneta alla fine del 700*, Florence, 1956; Gianfranco Torcellan, *Una figura della Venezia settecentesca. Andrea Memmo*, Venice–Rome, 1963.

However, it is a significant exception when considered in relation to what was happening at that time on the continent. We cannot explain the situation by observing that the British are a unique people. Britain gains, I would say, by being studied in the light of the history of the other European states of the eighteenth century. The comparison is still more important as the seventies and the eighties throughout Europe saw the beginning of the age of great reforms, and of the reactions they aroused. The age of Turgot and of Joseph II also witnessed the economic expansion of three decades being replaced by a period of uncertainty and of abrupt fluctuations of the economy. Moreover, reforms are expensive, and under this burden even small masterpieces of Enlightened reform, such as the Tuscany of Pietro Leopoldo, ended by finding themselves in difficulties after twenty-five years of work.

These years before the French revolution witnessed first of all, far away on the outermost limits, the insurrection and revolt of the Corsicans, Pugačev and the American colonies. They were so distant as hardly to seem to bear on Europe. But the renewed activity of the absolutist states, the struggle against the local bodies, the rapid growth, through the new juntas and commissions, and the ever greater development of central administration gave rise to increasingly serious conflicts with the parliaments in France, with the traditional autonomies in Austrian Flanders, with the nobility in Hungary, and, finally, even with that governing class which had come to power at the end of the sixties in Milan, just as they did with the local autonomies in Catalonia and with the Inquisition in Spain. The work of the centralized state was opposed by the most diverse forces; regional autonomies, and, even at this early date, by the ideal of a constitutional freedom, as well as by a new spirit of independence which found its model in distant America. The tension between utopia and reform increased everywhere—in the Naples of Filangieri and Pagano, in Russia where Aleksandr Radiščev, the first figure of the new intelligentsia, was emerging, in the Spain of Jovellanos and Goya. It was present in France where Raynal, Brissot de Warville, Mably and, once again, Diderot were developing the language of revolution, where the yearning for a new world took on aberrant and pathological forms, resembling that mesmerism so lucidly described recently by

Robert Darnton.[1] A sharp economic crisis, after the many survived by the old regime, was enough to precipitate a revolution.

With the participation in the American war and with the revolt in the United Provinces the circle of revolution had been closing round France. In 1789, it reached the home of the Enlightenment.

[1] Robert Darnton, *Mesmerism and the end of the Enlightenment in France*, Cambridge, Mass., 1968.

BIBLIOGRAPHY

Absoljutizm v Rossii (*XVII–XVIII* vv.). Edited by N. M. Družinin. Moscow, 1964.

Accinelli, Francesco Maria. *La verità risvegliata, con tre dissertazioni della decadenza dell'Impero, della libertà di Genova, della soggezione di S. Remo alla Repubblica.* MS. Berio library, Genoa.

Akademija nauk SSSR. *Iz istorii social'no-političeskich idej. Sbornik statej k semidesjatipjatiletiju Ak. V. P. Volgina.* Moscow, 1955.

Istorija socialističeskich učenij. Moscow, 1962.

Alembert, Jean Le Rond d'. *Essai sur la société des gens de lettres et des grands, sur la réputation, sur les mécènes et sur les récompenses littéraires* in *idem*, *Mélanges de littérature, d'histoire et de philosophie*, vol. 2. Berlin, 1753.

Allen, Robert Joseph. *The clubs of Augustan London.* Cambridge, Mass., 1933.

Althusser, Louis. *Montesquieu. La politique et l'histoire.* Paris, 1959.

Anderson, George Pomeroy. 'Pascal Paoli, an inspiration to the sons of liberty' in *Massachusetts historical society. Proceedings*, vol. XXVI.

Ansaldi, Giovanni. *A tutto l'ordine fortissimo, fedelissimo, generosissimo che intende reprimer le insolenze e ripararsi dalle ingiustitie di quelli che male operano e male governano in Genova, salute e aviso.* N.p., 1628.

Verità esaminata a favor del popolo, il quale con ingiustitia è tenuto fuori del governo di Genova contro alcuni tiranni dell'istesso popolo che già se ne credono impossessati con fraude. N.p., 1628.

Argenson, René-Louis Voyer d'. *Considérations sur le gouvernement ancien et présent de la France.* Yverdon, 1764.

Journal et mémoires. Edited by Edme-Jacques-Benoît Rathery. Paris, 1868.

Association internationale des études françaises. *Cahiers*, vol. II. Paris, 1952. *L'Encyclopédie et son rayonnement à l'étranger.*

Baczko, Bronisław. 'Le mot de l'énigme métaphysique ou Dom Deschamps' in *Cahiers Vilfredo Pareto*, no. 15. 1968.

Baden, Carl Friedrich von. *Brieflicher Verkehr mit Mirabeau und Du Pont.* Edited by Carl Knies. Heidelberg, 1892.

Bailyn, Bernard. *The ideological origins of the American revolution.* Cambridge, Mass., 1967.

Beccaria, Cesare. *Dei delitti e delle pene.* Harlem (Leghorn), 1764.

Dei delitti e delle pene. Con una raccolta di lettere e di documenti relativi alla nascita dell'opera e alla sua fortuna nell'Europa del Settecento. Edited by Franco Venturi. Turin, 1965.

Traité des délits et des peines, traduit de l'italien d'après la troisième édition, revue, corrigée et augmentée par l'auteur, avec des additions de l'auteur qui n'ont pas encore paru en italien. Lausanne (Paris), 1766.

Becker, Carl. *The heavenly city of the eighteenth-century philosophers.* New Haven, 1932.

Becker, Marvin B. *Florence in transition.* Baltimore, 1967 and 1968.

Bentley, Richard. *La friponnerie laïque des prêtendus esprits-forts d'Angleterre, ou remarques de Philéleuthère de Leipsick sur le Discours de la liberté de penser, traduites de l'Anglois sur la septième édition* par Mr. N. N. (i.e. A. Boisbeleau de la Chapelle). Amsterdam, 1738.

Remarks upon a late discourse of freethinking in a letter to G. H.[*are*]. London, 1713.

Berengo, Marino. *Nobili e mercanti nella Lucca del Cinquecento.* Turin, 1965.

La società veneta alla fine del '700. Florence, 1956.

Bertelli, Sergio. *Giannoniana. Autografi, manoscritti e documenti della fortuna di Pietro Giannone.* Milan–Naples, 1968.

Bollème, Geneviève; Ehrard, Jean; Furet, François; Roche, Daniel; Roger, Jacques. *Livre et société dans la France du XVIIIe siècle.* Post-face d'Alphonse Dupront. Paris–The Hague, 1965.

Booy, Jean Th. de. *Histoire d'un manuscrit de Diderot: 'La promenade d'un sceptique'.* Frankfurt-am-Main, 1964.

Boswell on the Grand Tour: Italy, Corsica and France. 1765–1766. Edited by F. Brady and F. A. Pottle. London, 1955.

Boulanger, Nicolas-Antoine. *Recherches sur l'origine du despotisme oriental. Ouvrage posthume de* Mr. *B.I.D.P.E.C.* (Geneva), 1761.

Bourde, André. *Agronomie et agronomes en France au XVIIIe siècle.* Paris, 1967.

Bourychkine, Paul. *Bibliographie sur la franc-maçonnerie en Russie, complétée et mise au point par Tatiana Bakounine.* Paris–The Hague, 1964.

Bouwsma, William J. *Venice and the defence of republican liberty. Renaissance values in the age of Counter-Reformation.* Berkeley, 1968.

Braubach, Max. *Geschichte und Abenteuer. Gestalten um den Prinzen Eugen.* Münich, 1950.

Brissot de Warville, Jacques-Pierre. *Recherches philosophiques sur le droit de propriété et sur le vol.* Chartres, 1780.

Théorie des lois criminelles. Berlin, 1781.

Brooks, Richard A. *A critical bibliography of French literature.* Vol. IV. *The eighteenth century. Supplement.* Syracuse, 1968.

Browne, Peter. *A letter in answer to a book entitled Christianity not mysterious.* Dublin, 1697.

Cantimori, Delio. *Il problema rinascimentale a proposito di Armando Sapori* in *Studi di storia.* Turin, 1959.

Valore dell'umanesimo. Ibid.

Capra, Carlo. *Giovanni Ristori da illuminista a funzionario. 1755–1830.* Florence, 1968.

Casini, Paolo. *L'universo macchina. Origini della filosofia newtoniana.* Bari, 1969.

Casoni, Filippo. *Storia del bombardamento di Genova nell'anno 1684,* edited by Achille Neri. Genoa, 1877.

Cassirer, Ernst. *Die Philosophie der Aufklärung.* Tübingen, 1932.

Cauz, Konstantin Franz de. *De cultibus magicis.* Vienna, 1767.

Cobban, Alfred. *Ambassadors and secret agents. The diplomacy of the first earl of Malmesbury at the Hague.* London, 1954.

The role of the Enlightenment in modern history. In search of humanity. London, 1960.

Coe, Richard N. *Morelly. Ein Rationalist auf dem Wege zum Sozialismus.* Berlin, 1961.

Colligan, Hay J. *The Arian movement in England.* Manchester, 1913.

Collins, Anthony. *Discours sur la liberté de penser. Écrit à l'occasion d'une nouvelle secte d'esprits forts. Traduit de l'anglois et augmenté d'une lettre d'un médecin arabe.* London, 1714.

A discourse of free-thinking, occasion'd by the rise and growth of a sect call'd free-thinkers. London, 1713.

The commonwealths man unmasqu'd, or a just rebuke to the author of the Account of Denmark. London, 1694.

Confino, Michael. *Domaines et seigneurs en Russie vers la fin du XVIIIe siecle. Étude de structures agraires et de mentalités économiques*. Paris, 1963.

Histoire et psychologie: à propos de la noblesse russe au XVIIIe siècle in *Annales*, 1963.

Cozzi, Gaetano. *Il doge Nicolò Contarini*. Venice–Rome, 1958.

Politica e diritto nella riforma del diritto penale veneto nel Settecento. Padua, 1966–7.

Cragg, G. R. *From Puritanism to the age of reason. A study of changes in religious thought within the Church of England, 1660–1700*. Cambridge 1950.

Dacier, André. *Œuvres d'Horace*. Paris, 1727.

Dakin, Douglas. *Turgot and the 'Ancien régime' in France*. London, 1939.

Dalin, V. M. *Grakch Babef nakanune i vo vremja Velikoj francuzskoj revoljucii (1785–1794)*. Moscow, 1963.

Darbishire, Helen (ed.). *The early lives of Milton*. London, 1934.

Darnton, Robert. *Mesmerism and the end of the Enlightenment in France*. Cambridge, Mass., 1968.

Davanzati, Bernardo. *A discourse upon coins, being publickly spoken in the Academy (of Florence) anno 1588, translated out of the Italian by John Toland*. London, 1696.

Defourneaux, Marcelin. *Pablo Olavide ou l'afrancesado (1725–1803)*. Paris, 1959.

Deleyre, Alexandre. *Analyse de la philosophie du chancelier Bacon*. Paris, 1755.

Éloge de M. Roux, docteur-régent et professeur de chymie à la Faculté de Paris. Amsterdam, 1777.

'Épingle' in *Encyclopédie*, vol. v.

Essai sur la vie de M. Thomas. Paris, 1791.

'Fanatisme' in *Encyclopédie*, vol. VI.

Idées sur l'éducation nationale. Paris (Convention nationale), n.d.

Opinion sur la question du jugement de Louis XVI. Paris (Convention nationale), n.d.

'Pensées d'un républicain sur les mœurs de ce siècle' in *Journal encyclopédique*, October 1758.

Revue des feuilles de M. Fréron. London (Paris), 1756.

Tableau de l'Europe pour servir de supplément à l'Histoire philosophique des établissements et du commerce des Européens dans les deux Indes. Maestricht, 1774.

Deschamps, dom Léger-Marie. *Prawdziwy system, czyli rozwiązanie zagadki metafisyki i moralności.* Edited by Bronisław Baczko. Warsaw, 1967.

Le vrai système, ou le mot de l'énigme métaphysique et morale. Edited by Jean Thomas and Franco Venturi. Geneva, 1939 and 1963.

Desing, Anselm. *Juris naturae larva detracta compluribus libris sub titulo juris naturae prodeuntibus, ut puffendorffianis, heineccianis, wolffianis etc.* Munich, 1753.

Diaz, Furio. *Filosofia e politica nel Settecento francese.* Turin, 1962.

Francesco Maria Gianni dalla burocrazia alla politica sotto Pietro Leopoldo di Toscana. Milan–Naples, 1966.

Dickson, Peter G. M. *The financial revolution in England. A study in the development of public credit. 1688–1755.* London–New York, 1967.

Diderot, Denis. *Correspondance.* Edited by Georges Roth. Paris, 1955.

Lettre sur les aveugles à l'usage de ceux qui voient. London (Paris), 1749.

Mémoires pour Cathérine II. Edited by Paul Vernière. Paris, 1966.

Observations sur le Nakaz in *Œuvres politiques.* Edited by Paul Vernière. Paris, 1963.

Œuvres complètes. Edited by J. Assézat and M. Tourneax. Paris, 1875.

Œuvres politiques. Edited by Paul Vernière. Paris, 1963.

Pensées philosophiques. Paris, 1746.

*Principes de la philosophie morale, ou essai de M. S**** [Shaftesbury] *sur le mérite et la vertu. Avec réflexions.* Amsterdam, 1745.

La promenade du sceptique in *Œuvres complètes.* Vol. I. Edited by J. Assézat. Paris, 1875.

Réfutation suivie de l'ouvrage d'Helvétius intitulé 'L'homme' in *Œuvres complètes.* Vol. II. Edited by J. Assézat. Paris, 1875.

Supplément au voyage de Bougainville ou Dialogue entre A. et B. in *Œuvres philosophiques.* Edited by Paul Vernière. Paris, 1961.

Disraeli, Benjamin, earl of Beaconsfield. *Contarini Fleming. A psychological auto-biography.* London, 1832.

Donvez, Jacques, 'Diderot, Aiguillon et Vergennes' in *Revue des sciences humaines.* New series, no. 87. July–September 1957.

Doria, Paolo Mattia. *La vita civile.* Naples, 1710.

Dukes, Paul. *Catherine the Great and the Russian nobility.* Cambridge, 1967.

Dulac, Georges. 'Une lettre de Diderot à Turgot' in *Studi francesi,* no. 36. September–December 1968.

Elliot, J. H. *The revolt of the Catalans.* Cambridge, 1963.

D'Estrées, Victor-Marie. *Letters.* British Museum, Add. MSS. 4282.

Fabre, Jean. *Stanislas-Auguste Poniatowski et l'Europe des lumières.* Paris, 1952.

Facchinei, Ferdinando. *Note e osservazioni sul libro intitolato Dei delitti e delle pene.* n.p. [Venice], 1765.

Ferguson, Adam. *An essay on the history of civil society. 1767.* Edited by Duncan Forbes. Edinburgh, 1966.

Fink, Zera S. *The classical republicans. An essay in the recovery of a pattern of thought in seventeenth-century England.* Evanston, 1945.

Firpo, Luigi. 'Contributi ad un dizionario storico. Ancora a proposito di *Sapere aude*' in *Rivista storica italiana,* no. I, 1960.

'Contributo alla bibliografia del Beccaria (Le edizioni italiane settecentesche del *Dei delitti e delle pene*)' in *Atti del convegno internazionale su Cesare Beccaria promosso dall'Accademia delle scienze di Torino.* Turin, 1966.

Forbes, Duncan. 'Scientific whiggism. Adam Smith and John Millar' in *Cambridge Journal,* no. III. 1954.

Foscarini, Marco. *Della letteratura veneziana libri otto.* Padua, 1752.

'Storia arcana ed altri scritti inediti' in *Archivio storico italiano,* vol. V. 1843.

Galante Garrone, Alessandro. *Buonarroti e Babeuf.* Turin, 1948.

Galiani, Ferdinando. *Della moneta libri cinque.* Naples, 1750 (1751) and 1780.

Garosci, Aldo. *San Marino, mito e storiografia tra i libertini e il Carducci.* Milan, 1967.

Sul concetto di 'borghesia'. Verifica storica di un saggio crociano in *Miscellanea Walter Maturi.* Turin, 1966.

Gay, Peter. *The Enlightenment: An interpretation.* New York, 1967 and 1969.

Voltaire's politics. The poet as realist. Princeton, 1959.

Genovesi, Antonio. *Delle lezioni di commercio o sia d'economia civile da leggersi nella cattedra intieriana.* Naples, 1765 (1766)–7.

Geyl, Pieter. *Revolutiedagen te Amsterdam (augustus–september 1748). Prins Willem IV en de Doelistenbeweging.* The Hague, 1936.

Giannone, Pietro. *Il triregno.* Edited by Alfredo Parente. Bari, 1940.

I giornali giacobini italiani. Edited by Renzo de Felice. Milan, 1962.

Girsberger, H. *Der utopische Sozialismus des XVIII. Jahrhunderts in Frankreich und seine philosophischen und materiellen Grundlagen.* Leipzig, 1924.

Goldman, Lucien. *L'Illuminismo e la società moderna. Storia e funzione attuale dei valori di libertà, eguaglianza, tolleranza.* Turin, 1967.

Gorani, Giuseppe. *Il vero dispotismo.* London (Geneva), 1770.

Gordon, Lev Semionovič. 'Nekotorye itogi izučenija zapreščennoj literatury epochi prosveščenija' (Vtoraja polovina, XVIII v.) in *Francuzskij eżegodnik.* 1959.

Goudar, Ange. *Histoire générale de la révolution de Gênes, contenant tout ce qui s'est passé dans cette République depuis la mort de Charles VI jusqu'à la levée du siège par les Allemans.* British Museum, Add. MSS. 17 395.

Les intérêts de la France mal entendus dans les branches de l'agriculture, de la population, des finances, du commerce, de la marine et de l'industrie, par un citoyen. Amsterdam, 1756.

Naples, ce qu'il faut faire pour rendre ce royaume florissant. Amsterdam, 1771.

Grimm, M. *et al. Correspondance littéraire.* Edited by Maurice Tourneux. Paris, 1878.

Grimsley, Ronald. *Jean d'Alembert. 1717–1783.* Oxford, 1963.

Gunn, John A. W. *Politics and the public interest in the seventeenth century.* London–Toronto, 1969.

Hamilton, Earl J. *The mercantilism of Gerónimo de Uztáriz: a reëxamination* in *Economics, sociology and the modern world.* Edited by Norman Edwin Himes. Cambridge, Mass., 1935.

Harrington, James. *Oceana and his other works, some whereof are now first published from his own manuscripts. The whole collected, methodiz'd and review'd, with the exact account of life prefix'd, by John Toland.* London, 1700.

Hart, Jeffrey. *Viscount Bolingbroke, tory humanist.* London–Toronto, 1965.

Hartung, Fritz and Mousnier, Roland. *Quelques problèmes concernant la monarchie absolue* in *X Congresso internazionale di scienze storiche. Relazioni*, vol. IV. *Storia moderna.* Florence, 1955.

Heath, James. *Eighteenth-century penal theory.* Oxford, 1963.

Heinemann, Friedrich Heinrich. 'John Toland and the age of Enlightenment' in *Review of English Studies*, no. 78. 1944.

'Toland and Leibniz' in *The Philosophical Review.* 1945.

Helvétius, Claude-Adrien. *De l'homme, de ses facultés intellectuelles et de son éducation.* Amsterdam, 1775.

Herder, Johann Gottfried. *Versuch einer Geschichte der lyrischen Dichtkunst* in *Sämtliche Werke*, vol. 32. Edited by Bernard Suphan. Berlin, 1891.

Herr, Richard. *The eighteenth century revolution in Spain.* Princeton, 1958.

Hert [Hertius], J. N. *De socialitate primo naturalis juris principio dissertatio* in *idem*, *Commentationum atque opusculorum de selectis et rarioribus ex jurisprudentia universali, publica, feudali et romana nec non historia germanica argumentis tomi tres.* Frankfurt-am-Main, 1700.

Hill, Christopher. 'Republicanism after the Restoration' in *New Left Review*, no. III. 1960.

Himes, Norman Edwin (ed.). *Economics, sociology and the modern world.* Cambridge, Mass., 1935.

History of Poland. Edited by A. Gieysztor, S. Kieniewicz, E. Rostworowski, J. Tazbir, H. Wereszycki. Warsaw, 1968.

Holbach, Paul-Henry Thiry d'. *Le christianisme dévoilé, ou examen des principes et des effets de la religion chrétienne.* (Nancy?), 1761.

Hovy, Johannes. *Het voorstel van 1751 tot instelling van een beperkt vrijhavenstelsel in de Republiek.* Groningen, 1966.

Huber, Ulrich. *De iure popularis, optimatium et regalis imperii sine vi et a sui juris populo constituti.* 1689.

Hume, David. *Essays and treatises on several subjects.* London, 1753–6.

Illuministi italiani, tomo III. *Riformatori lombardi, piemontesi e toscani.* Edited by F. Venturi. Milan–Naples, 1958.

Tomo V. *Riformatori napoletani.* Edited by F. Venturi. Milan–Naples, 1962.

Tomo VII. *Riformatori delle antiche repubbliche, dei ducati, dello Stato pontificio e delle isole.* Edited by G. Giarrizzo, G. Torcellan, and F. Venturi. Milan–Naples, 1965.

Institut national d'études démographiques. *François Quesnay et la physiocratie.* Paris, 1958.

Jablonowski, Horst. 'Die geistige Bewegung in Russland in der zweiten Hälfte des 18. Jahrhunderts' in *Le mouvement des idées dans les pays slaves pendant la seconde moitié du XVIIIe siècle. Atti del Colloquio slavistico tenutosi ad Uppsala il 19–21 agosto 1960.* Rome, 1962.

Jobert, Ambroise. *Magnats polonais et physiocrates français (1764–1774).* Paris, 1941.

Journal d'économie publique, de morale et de politique, no. XXI. 'De la proprieté, de quelques philosophes qui l'ont attaquée et des hommes qui accusent de ces attaques tous les philosophes et la philosophie'. 30 ventôse, an V (20 March 1797).

Jovy, Ernest. 'Le précurseur et l'inspirateur direct des *Lettres persanes*' in *Bulletin du bibliophile.* Paris, 1917.

Kann, Robert A. *A study in Austrian intellectual history. From late Baroque to Romanticism.* New York, 1960.

Kohler, Johann David (ed.). *Historische Münz-Belustigung*, no. 47. 1740.

Konopczyński, Władysław. *Stanisław Konarski.* Warsaw, 1926.

Kossman, Ernst Heinrich. *La Fronde.* Leiden, 1954.

Politieke theorie in het zeventiende-eeuwse Nederland. Amsterdam, 1960.

Krauss, Werner. *Studien zur deutschen und französischen Aufklärung.* Berlin, 1963.

Kula, Witold. *Teoria economica del sistema feudale. Proposta d'un modello.* Turin, 1970.

Labrousse, C. E. *Esquisse du mouvement des prix et des revenus en France au XVIIIe siècle.* Paris, 1932.

La Court, Peter Cornelis de. *Anweisungen der heilsamen politischen Gründe und Maximen der Republicen Holland und West-Friesland.* Rotterdam, 1671.

Lane, Frederick C. 'At the roots of republicanism' in *American Historical Review*, no. 2. 1966.

Le Blanc, Jean-Bernard. *Lettres d'un François.* 2 vols. The Hague, 1745.

Lechler, Gotthard Victor. *Geschichte des Englischen Deismus.* Stuttgart–Tübingen, 1841.

Lefebvre, Georges. *La grande peur de 1789.* Paris, 1932.

'Le mouvement des prix et les origines de la Révolution française' in *Annales d'histoire économique et sociale*, vol. IX. 1937.

Les paysans du Nord pendant la Révolution française. Lille, 1924 and Bari, 1959.

Lehmann, William C. *John Millar of Glasgow, 1735–1801. His life and his contribution to sociological analysis.* Cambridge, 1960.

Leibniz, Wilhelm Gottfried. *Correspondance avec l'électrice Sophie de Brunswick-Lunebourg.* Edited by Onno Klopp. Hanover, n.d.

Leśnodorski, Bogusław. *Les jacobins polonais.* Paris, 1965.

Polscy jakobini. Warsaw, 1960.

Leszczyński, Stanislas. *La voix libre du citoyen, ou observations sur le gouvernement de la Pologne.* N.p., 1749.

Lichtenberger, A. *Le socialisme au XVIIIe siècle. Étude sur les idées socialistes dans les écrivains français du XVIIIe siècle avant la Révolution.* Paris, 1895.

Linguet, Simon-Nicolas-Henry. 'Fragment d'une lettre à l'auteur du Traité des délits et des peines' in *Journal œconomique.* April 1770.

Lipiński, Edward. *De Copernic à Stanislas Leszczyński. La pensée économique et démographique en Pologne.* Paris–Warsaw, 1961.

La Lorraine dans l'Europe des lumières. Actes du colloque organisé par la Faculté des lettres et des sciences humaines de l'Université de Nancy (24–27 ottobre 1966). Nancy, 1968.

Lortholary Albert. *Le mirage russe en France au XVIIIe siècle.* Paris, 1951.

Lough, John. *Essays on the 'Encyclopédie' of Diderot and d'Alembert.* Oxford, 1968.

Lüthy, Herbert. *La banque protestante en France de la Révocation de l'Édit de Nantes à la Révolution*. Paris, 1959–61.

Mably, Gabriel Bonnot de. *De la législation ou principes des lois*. Amsterdam, 1776.

Maestro, Marcello. *Voltaire and Beccaria as reformers of criminal law*. New York, 1942.

Maffei, Scipione. *Il consiglio politico alla Repubblica veneta*. A cura di L. Messedaglia. Verona, 1955.

Magnanima, Luca. *Lettere italiane sopra la Corsica*. Lausanne (Leghorn), 1770.

Manuel, Frank E. *The eighteenth century confronts the gods*. Cambridge, Mass., 1959.

Marana, Giovanni Paolo. *La congiura di Raffaello della Torre con le mosse della Savoia contro la Repubblica di Genova, libri due*. Lyons, 1682.

Dialogue de Gênes et d'Algers, villes foudroyées par les armes invincibles de Louis le Grand l'année 1684. Amsterdam, 1685.

L'espion dans les cours des princes chrétiens, 12th ed. Cologne, 1700.

Mars, Francis L. 'Ange Goudar cet inconnu' in *Casanova Gleanings*, no. 9. 1966.

Mathias, Peter. *The first industrial nation. An economic history of Britain. 1700–1914*. London, 1969.

Matilla Tascón, Antonio. *La única contribución y el catasto de La Ensenada*. Madrid, 1947.

Matteucci, Nicola. *Jacques Mallet-Du Pan*. Naples, 1957.

Maupertuis, Pierre-Louis Moreau de. *Œuvres. Nouvelle édition corrigée et augmentée*. Lyon. 1756.

Merker, Nicolao. *L'illuminismo tedesco. Età di Lessing*. Bari, 1968.

Merriman, Roger Bigelow. *Six contemporaneous revolutions*. Oxford, 1938.

Michalski, Jerzy. 'Problem *ius agratiandi* i kary śmierci w Polsce w latach siedemdziesiątych XVIII w.' in *Czasopismo prawno-historyczne*, vol. x, no. 2. 1958.

Mirabeau, Victor Riqueti de. *L'ami des hommes ou Traité de la population*. Avignon, 1756–8.

Théorie de l'impôt. The Hague, 1760.

Molesworth, Robert. *An account of Denmark as it was in the year 1692*. London, 1694.

Letters. Public Record Office, 30/24/20/137.

Molnar, Erik. *Les fondements économiques et sociaux de l'absolutisme* in *XIIe Congrès international des sciences historiques. Rapports*, vol. IV, *Méthodologie et histoire contemporaine*. Vienna, 1965.

Momigliano, Arnaldo. *Contributo alla storia degli studi classici*. Rome, 1955, 1960, 1966, 1969.

'Gli studi classici di Scipione Maffei' in *Giornale storico della letteratura italiana*, no. 403. 1956.

Montesquieu, Charles-Louis de Secondat de. *Esprit des lois* in *Œuvres complètes*, vol. I. Edited by André Masson. Paris, 1950.

Lettres persanes. Texte établi, avec introduction, bibliographie, notes et relevé de variantes par Paul Vernière. Paris, 1960.

Morelly. *Code de la nature*. Edited by Gilbert Chinard. Paris, 1950.

Morrison, Christian. *La place de Forbonnais dans la pensée économique* in Morrison, Christian and Goffin, Robert, *Questions financières aux XVIIIe et XIXe siècles*. Paris, 1967.

Mortier, Roland. *Diderot en Allemagne. 1750–1850*. Paris, 1954.

Moser, Friedrich Karl von. *Geschichte der päbstlichen Nuntien in Deutschland*. Frankfurt–Leipzig, 1788.

Moyle, Walter, *Essai sur le gouvernement de Rome. Traduit de l'anglais. Ouvrage utile aux hommes d'état et aux philosophes*. Paris, an X/1801.

The works, none of which were ever before publish'd. London, 1726.

Müller, Hans. *Ursprung und Geschichte des Wortes 'Sozialismus' und seiner Verwandten*. Hanover, 1967.

Naylor, John F. *The British aristocracy and the Peerage Bill of 1719*. Oxford, 1969.

Palmer, R. R. *The age of democratic revolution: a political history of Europe and America, 1760–1800*. I, *The challenge*. II, *The struggle*. Princeton, 1959 and 1964.

Parente, Fausto. 'Il contributo di Luigi Salvatorelli alla storia di Israele e del cristianesimo antico' in *Rivista storica italiana*, no. III. 1966.

Parker, Harold Talbot. *The cult of antiquity ond the French revolution-*

aries. A study in the development of the revolutionary spirit. Chicago, 1937.

Perry, Thomas W. *Public opinion, propaganda and politics in eighteenth-century England. A study of the Jew Bill of 1753.* Cambridge, Mass., 1967.

Pidou de Saint-Olon. *Papers.* Bibliothèque de l'Arsenal, MSS. 760, 6546 and 6613.

Pilati, Carlantonio. *Di una riforma d'Italia ossia dei mezzi di riformare i più cattivi costumi e le più perniciose leggi d'Italia.* Villafranca (Chur), 1767.

Plumard de Dangeul (pseud. John Nickolls). *Remarques sur les avantages et les désavantages de la France et de la Grande Bretagne.* Leyden, 1754.

Plumb, J. H. *The growth of political stability in England. 1675–1725.* London, 1967.

Pocock, J. G. A. *The ancient constitution and feudal law. English historical thought in the seventeenth century.* Cambridge, 1957.

Prideaux, Humphrey. *Letters of Humphrey Prideaux sometime dean of Norwich to John Ellis sometime under-secretary of state. 1674–1722.* Edited by Edward Maunde Thompson. London, 1875.

Procacci, Giuliano. *Studi sulla fortuna di Machiavelli.* Rome, 1965.

Proust, Jacques. *Diderot et l'Encyclopédie.* Paris, 1967.

Quesnay, François. 'Fermiers' in *Encyclopédie*, vol. VI.

'Grains' *in Encyclopédie*, vol. VII.

Scritti economici. Edited by Renato Zangheri. Bologna, 1966.

Raab, Felix. *The English face of Machiavelli. A changing interpretation. 1500–1700.* London–Toronto, 1964.

Radbruch, Gustav. *Elegantiae juris criminalis. Vierzehn Studien zur Geschichte des Strafrechts.* Basle, 1950.

Radzinowicz, Leon. *A history of criminal law and its administration from 1750.* I, *The movement for reform.* London, 1948.

Raeff, Marc. *Origins of the Russian intelligentsia. The eighteenth-century nobility.* New York, 1966.

Ricuperati, Giuseppe. 'Libertinismo e deismo a Vienna: Spinoza, Toland e il *Triregno*' in *Rivista storica italiana*, no. 2. 1967.

'Studi recenti su Bayle' in *Rivista storica italiana*, no. 2. 1968.

Ries, Paul. 'Robert Molesworth's *Account of Denmark.* A study in the art of political publishing and bookselling in England and the continent before 1700' in *Scandinavica*, vol. VII, no. 2. November 1968.

Robbins, Caroline. *The eighteenth-century commonwealthman. Studies in the transmission, development and circumstance of English liberal thought from the restoration of Charles II until the war with the Thirteen Colonies.* Cambridge, Mass., 1959.

(ed.). *Two English republican tracts. Plato redivivus or a Dialogue concerning government by Henry Neville. An essay upon the constitution of Roman government by Walter Moyle.* Cambridge, 1969.

Roche, Daniel. 'La diffusion des lumières. Un exemple: l'Académie de Châlons-sur-Marne' in *Annales*, no. V. 1964.

Roorda, Daniel J. *The ruling classes in Holland in the seventeenth century* in *Britain and the Netherlands.* Edited by J. S. Bromley and E. H. Kossman. Groningen, 1964.

Rosa, Mario. *Dispotismo e libertà nel Settecento. Interpretazioni repubblicane di Machiavelli.* Bari, 1964.

Rostworowski, Emanuel. *The Commonwealth of the gentry* in *History of Poland.* Edited by A. Gieysztor, S. Kieniewicz, E. Rostworowski, J. Tazbir, H. Wereszycki. Warsaw, 1968.

'Républicanisme sarmate et les lumières' in *Studies on Voltaire and the eighteenth century*, vols. XXIV–XXVII. 1963.

'Stanislas Leszczyński et l'idée de la paix générale' in *La Lorraine dans l'Europe des lumières. Actes du colloque organisé par la Faculté des lettres et des sciences humaines de l'Université de Nancy (24–27 octobre 1966).* Nancy, 1968.

'La Suisse et la Pologne au XVIIIe siècle' in *Échanges entre la Pologne et la Suisse du XIVe au XIXe siècle.* Geneva, 1964.

'Voltaire et la Pologne' in *Studies on Voltaire and the eighteenth century*, vol. LXII. 1968.

Rothkrug, Lionel. *Opposition to Louis XIV. The political and social origins of the French Enlightenment.* Princeton, 1965.

Rotta, Salvatore. 'Documenti per la storia dell'illuminismo a Genova. Lettere di Agostino Lomellini a Paolo Frisi' in *Miscellanea di storia ligure*, vol. I, 1958.

Rousseau, Jean-Jacques, *Considérations sur le gouvernement de Pologne* in *idem, Œuvres complètes.* III. *Du contrat social. Écrits politiques.* Paris, 1964.

Correspondance complète. Edited by R. A. Leigh, Geneva, 1965 ff.

Correspondance générale. Edited by T. Dufour. Paris, 1924 ff.

Discours sur l'origine et les fondemens de l'inégalité parmi les hommes. Amsterdam, 1755.

Du contract social ou principes du droit politique. Amsterdam, 1762.

Lettres écrites de la montagne. Amsterdam, 1764.

Œuvres complètes. Edited by Bernard Gagnebin and Marcel Raymond. III, *Du contrat social. Écrits politiques.* Paris, 1964.

Projet de constitution de la Corse. in *idem, Œuvres complètes.* III, *Du contrat social. Écrits politiques.* Paris, 1964.

Rudé, George. *The crowd in history. 1740–1848.* New York–London, 1964.

Wilkes and Liberty. A social study of 1763 to 1774. Oxford, 1962.

Saint-Pierre, Charles-Irénée Castel de. *Projet de traité pour rendre la paix perpétuelle entre les souverains chrétiens.* Utrecht, 1716.

Saitta, Armando. *Filippo Buonarroti.* Rome, 1960.

Salvatorelli, Luigi. 'From Locke to Reizenstein. The historical investigation of the origins of Christianity' in *The Harvard Theological Review.* 1929.

Sarrailh, Jean. *L'Espagne éclairée de la seconde moitié du XVIIIe siècle.* Paris, 1954.

Ščerbatov, M. M. *Sočinenija.* Edited by I. P. Chruščov. St Petersburg, 1898.

Schlenke, Manfred. *England und das friderizianische Preussen. 1740–1763. Ein Beitrag zum Verhältnis von Politik und öffentlicher Meinung im England des 18. Jahrhunderts.* Munich. 1963.

Schoffer, I. 'Did Holland's golden age coincide with a period of crisis?' in *Acta historiae nederlandica*, vol. I. Leiden, 1966.

Seznec, Jean. *Essai sur Diderot et l'antiquité.* Paris, 1957.

Shackleton, Robert. *Montesquieu. A critical biography.* Oxford, 1961.

Shafer, Robert Jones. *The Economic Societies in the Spanish world (1763–1821).* Syracuse, 1958.

Shaftesbury, Anthony Ashley Cooper, 3rd earl of. *Characteristicks, oder Schilderungen von Menschen, Sitten und Zeiten, aus dem Englischen übersetzt.* Leipzig, 1768.

Characteristicks of men, manners, opinions, times. London, 1711.

Smart, Alastair. *The life and art of Allan Ramsay*. London, 1952.

Soboul, Albert. *Les sansculottes parisiens en l'an II. Mouvement populaire et gouvernement révolutionnaire, 2 juin 1793–9 thermidor an II*. Paris, 1958.

Spengler, Joseph J. *Économie et population. Les doctrines françaises avant 1800. De Budé a Condorcet*. Paris, 1954.

Spinoza, Baruch. *Trattato politico*. Edited by Antonio Droetto. Turin, 1958.

Spurlin, Paul M. 'Beccaria's essay On crimes and punishments in eighteenth-century America' in *Studies on Voltaire and the eighteenth century*, vol. XXVII. 1963.

Stegmann, Ildefons. *Anselm Desing Abt von Ensdorf. 1669–1772. Ein Beitrag zur Geschichte der Aufklärung in Bayern*. Munich, 1929.

Sterlich, Romualdo. *Letters to Giovanni Bianchi*. Biblioteca Gambalunga. Rimini. Fondo Gambetti.

Suite des révolutions hollandoises ou le Rétablissement des rois de Frize. N.p. 1747.

Svodnyj katalog russkoj knigi graždanskoj pečati XVIII veka. 1725–1800. Moscow, 1962–6.

Tabacco, Giovanni. *Andrea Tron (1712–1785) e la crisi dell'aristocrazia senatoria a Venezia*. Trieste, 1957.

Thorschmid, Urban Gottlob. *Vollständige Engelländische Freydenker-Bibliothek*. Cassel, 1766.

Tinker, Chauncey Brewster. *A new nation* in *Nature's simple plan. A phase of radical thought in mid-eighteenth century*. Princeton, 1922.

Tisserand, Roger. *Les concurrents de J.-J. Rousseau à l'Académie de Dijon pour le prix de 1754*. Paris, 1936.

Toland, John. *Adeisidaemon, sive Titus Livius a superstitione vindicatus*. The Hague, 1709.

Christianity not mysterious, or a Treatise shewing that there is nothing in the Gospel contrary to reason nor above it and that no Christian doctrine can be properly call'd a mystery. London, 1696.

Clito. A poem on the force of eloquence. London, 1700.

Letters. British Museum, Add. MSS. 4295.

Nazarenus, or Jewish, Gentile and Mahometan Christianity. London, 1718.

Pantheisticon, sive formula celebrandae sodalitatis Socraticae. London, 1720.

Relation des cours de Prusse et de Hanovre. The Hague, 1706.

Vindicius Liberius or Mr Toland's defence of himself against the late lower House of Convocation and others. London, 1702.

Torcellan, Gianfranco. 'Cesare Beccaria a Venezia' in *Rivista storica italiana,* no. 3. 1964.

Una figura della Venezia settecentesca. Andrea Memmo. Venice–Rome, 1963.

Trevor-Roper, Hugh Redwald. *Religion, the Reformation and social change and other essays.* London, 1967.

Trinius, Johann Anton. *Freydenker-Lexikon.* Leipzig and Bernburg, 1759. (Turin 1960. Edited by Franco Venturi.)

Troyer, Howard William. *Ned Ward of Grubstreet. A study of sub-literary London in the eighteenth century.* Cambridge, Mass., 1946.

Tucker, J. E. The *Turkish Spy* and its French background' in *Revue de littérature comparée.* 1958.

Uztáriz, Gerónimo de. *Théorica y práctica de comercio y de marina.* Madrid, 1724, 1742, 1757.

Valjavec, Fritz. *Geschichte der abendländischen Aufklärung.* Vienna–Munich, 1961.

Venetiaansche berichten over de Vereenigde Nederlanden van 1660–1795. Edited by P. J. Blok. The Hague, 1909.

Venturi, Franco. 'Contributi ad un dizionario storico. "Was ist Aufklärung? *Sapere aude*"' in *Rivista storica italiana,* no. 1. 1959.

'Un enciclopedista: Alexandre Deleyre' in *Rivista storica italiana,* no. 4. 1965.

'La fortuna di Dom Deschamps' in *Cahiers Vilfredo Pareto,* no. 11. 1967.

'Galiani tra enciclopedisti e fisiocrati' in *Rivista storica italiana,* no. 1. 1960.

L'illuminismo nel Settecento europeo in *XIe Congrès international des sciences historiques. Rapports.* IV. *Histoire moderne.* Göteborg–Stockholm–Uppsala, 1960.

'L'immagine della Giustizia' in *Rivista storica italiana,* no. 3. 1964.

Jeunesse de Diderot. De 1713 à 1753. Paris, 1939.

Le origini dell'Enciclopedia. Turin, 1963.

'Postille inedite di Voltaire ad alcune opere di Nicolas-Antoine Boulanger e del barone d'Holbach' in *Studi francesi*, no. 2. 1958.

'Quelques notes sur le rapport de Horst Jablonowski' in *Le mouvement des idées dans les pays slaves pendant la seconde moitié du XVIIIe siècle. Atti del colloquio slavistico tenutosi ad Uppsala il 19–21 agosto 1960*. Rome, 1962.

Saggi sull'Europa illuminista. I. *Alberto Radicati di Passerano*. Turin, 1954.

Settecento riformatore. Da Muratori a Beccaria. Turin, 1969.

'"Socialista" e "socialismo" nell'Italia del Settecento' in *Rivista storica italiana*, no. 1. 1963.

Vernière, Paul. *Spinoza et la pensée française avant la Révolution*. Paris, 1954.

Verri, Pietro. *Considerazioni sul commercio dello Stato di Milano*. Edited by C. A. Vianello. Milan, 1939.

Meditazioni sulla felicità. Leghorn, 1763.

Vicens Vives, José. *Estructura administrativa estatal en los siglos XVI y XVII* in *XIe Congrès international des sciences historiques. Rapports*. IV, *Histoire moderne*. Stockholm, 1960.

Manual de historia económica de España. Barcelona, 1959.

Villari, Rosario. *La rivolta antispagnola a Napoli. Le origini (1585–1647)*. Bari, 1967.

Vitale, Vito. *Breviario della storia di Genova*. Genoa, 1955.

Voltaire, François-Marie Arouet de. *A.B.C., dialogue curieux traduit de l'Anglais de monsieur Huet*. (Geneva), 1762 (1768).

Commentaire sur le Traité des délits et des peines. Geneva, 1766.

Correspondence. Edited by T. Besterman. Geneva, 1953–

Idées républicaines par un membre d'un corps. (Geneva, 1765).

Vries, Johannes de. *De economische achteruitgang der Republiek in de achttiende eeuw*. Amsterdam. 1959.

Wade, Ira O. *The clandestine organisation and diffusion of philosophic ideas in France from 1700 to 1750*. Princeton, 1938.

'The search for a new Voltaire. Studies in Voltaire based upon material deposited at the American Philosophical Society' in *Transactions of the American Philosophical Society*. New Series, vol. XLVIII, pt. 4. July 1958.

The Wentworth Papers, 1705–1739. Selected from the private and family correspondence of Thomas Wentworth, Lord Raby, created in 1711 Earl of Strafford, with a memoir and notes by James Joel Cartwright. London, 1883.

Wilbur, Earl Morse. *A history of unitarianism. Socinianism and its antecedents.* 2 vols. Cambridge, Mass., 1947.

Wilson, Charles. *Anglo-Dutch commerce and finance in the eighteenth century.* Cambridge, 1941 (reprinted 1966).

Profit and Power. A study of England and the Dutch wars. London, 1957.

Winter, Eduard. *Frühaufklärung. Der Kampf gegen den Konfessionalismus in Mittel- und Osteuropa und die deutsch-slawische Begegnung.* Berlin, 1966.

Der Josefinismus und seine Geschichte. Beiträge zur Geistesgeschichte Oesterreichs. 1740–1848. Brünn–Munich–Vienna, 1943.

Wołoszyński, Ryszard W. 'La Pologne vue par l'Europe au XVIIIe siècle' in *Acta Poloniae historica*, no. 11. 1965.

Polska w opiniach francuzów XVIII w. Warsaw, 1964.

Youngson, A. J. *The making of classical Edinburgh.* Edinburgh, 1968.

Zagorin, Perez. *A history of political thought in the English revolution.* London, 1954.

INDEX

INDEX

INDEX

INDEX

INDEX